Family Preservation

A Brief Therapy Workbook

Insoo Kim Berg

Edited and Introduced by
Evan George

BRIEF THERAPY

First Published April 1991
Reprinted May 1991
Reprinted with corrections February 1993
Published by BT Press
17 Avenue Mansions, Finchley Road, London NW3 7AX

Typeset by Alex Gollner in 10 on 12.5 point Goudy

ISBN 1 871 697 670

The Author

Insoo Kim Berg is the director and co-founder of BFTC in Milwaukee, Wisconsin. A native of Korea and educated in the U.S., she offers a balance between the Eastern and Western ways of finding solutions to human problems. She is a consultant to various community agencies and schools, and has lectured extensively in the U.S., Europe, the Far East and Australia.

She is an expert in working with multi-problem families, drug and alcohol abusers, the homeless and delinquent adolescents and their families.

Acknowledgments

Insoo Kim Berg showed me *Family Preservation* a year ago. She has since rewritten it. With the aid of the editing skills of Jeanne Sullivan, Kath Walker and especially Evan George, the book was reshaped, bringing out its special relevance to the United Kingdom. My thanks to all of them for making this edition possible.

Richard Gollner, Publisher
London, May 1991

Contents

Foreword

Everybody knows a lot about families since we all grew up in one. Yet, the more one knows, the less one seems to know. Every family seems the same, yet they are all different. The family is a wonderful institution that is the source of so much pride and yet so much shame; so strengthening, yet so draining; so nurturing, yet so demanding; so easy to understand, yet so confusing.

Welcome to the exciting, energising, painful and exhausting work with families: FBS. This work will be the most meaningful and challenging you have ever done and will ever do. It will stretch your mind, help you discover skills and strengths you did not know you had. You will love the work and curse the problems. I assure you that it will be anything but boring.

You will touch the lives of the families you work with in a way that is not possible to measure. The impact you will make on your clients may not be obvious immediately but your clients will feel empowered for having travelled a short distance of their lives with you as their guide.

This manual is designed to ease your pain a little, to increase your excitement about your work, and to help you to grow through your discovery of the amazing human spirit, both in yourself and the client.

This is written to be your guide as you wade through the mountain of information about the families you work with. It is written in a step-by-step fashion, in simple language with very little jargon and few technical terms. The case examples are all real and I have been involved in them, either directly or indirectly. There is no mystery to "therapy". When you follow these steps, you are doing "therapy" and providing treatment to families, even though you may be working with only one person in the family.

I am grateful to all the families who taught me about their incredible strengths and resilience in the midst of pain and suffering.

A special thanks to my colleagues: Steve de Shazer and Larry Hopwood who have been generous with their help and patience.

Insoo Kim Berg
Milwaukee, Wisconsin, April, 1991

Introduction

The history of work in the field of child protection has been punctuated by tragedies, from Mary Ellen Wilson in New York in the last century, through John O'Neil, Maria Colwell, Tyra Henry, Jasmine Beckford and Kimberley Carlile. There have of course been many more children who have died at the hands of their adult carers, but these particular children, amongst a number of others, are remembered because their deaths led to pressure of public opinion for something to be done. And things have been done. But without exception the response has been legalistic and administrative. New laws have been passed, old laws have been changed. Guidelines for inter-disciplinary cooperation have been formulated, and refined and refined again. We have Case Conferences, Child Protection Registers and Key Workers. A great deal of thought, and some research, has gone into identifying "risk factors" and recently guidelines for assessment have been published (DOH 1988). There must be no denying that this work has been useful. Indeed there is some evidence that lives are being saved. But none of this has helped a worker, allocated a child protection case, to know what to do and what not to do to bring about change in the relationship between the child, or children in question, and the family.

The Children Act 1989, centred as it is on the idea of parents and professionals working together, promises a new beginning. But, unless the professionals involved have a workable model of change, all they will be bringing to the partnership will be material help, resources, facilities, respite care and the like. While such help is important and necessary at times, to bring about change in the complex family problems which typify many of the families that the helper will encounter in this work, such help is not sufficient.

The expansion of knowledge about families where child abuse or neglect has occurred has served to challenge the old stereotypes which left abuse in middle-class, apparently respectable families largely unrecognised and now workers hesitate, rightly, to generalise about so-called abusive families. And yet despite the diversity of family type, most professionals agree that finding ways of working with families who are angry, feeling disempowered, feeling intruded upon, "unmotivated" and "resistant" is a key practice issue. Models of change, in order to have any validity for workers in this field must give professionals clear ideas about how to work with families who do not want to be worked with. Insoo Kim Berg's ideas about developing cooperation more than fit the bill and indeed in her book she suggests specific interventions to help the worker to cooperate with the family's "unique way of cooperating" (de Shazer 1984). So the basic criterion for judging a model in this field, is more than fulfiled, but beyond this the solution focussed model which she applies is empowering of clients and optimistic of outlook, both vital factors in an an area of work where clients and workers alike can be overwhelmed by the weight of difficulty pushing down, and where both can be left feeling hopeless and useless.

For most British readers one major difference of case-management is presented. The context within which the work that Insoo Kim Berg describes takes place, separates the primary child protection and treatment functions, leaving the Family Based worker free to concentrate primarily on the question of change, secure in the knowledge that child protection, in its most limited sense, is being handled by another agency. The potential for creativity of this model has been described elsewhere (Asen et al. 1989) but the majority of child protection workers in Britain have the double task, protection and treatment, to perform. Not only must every transaction with the family be evaluated in terms of "is this different?", "is this useful?", but also in terms of "could this be dangerous?" or "is this evidence of underlying pathology emerging?" The worker is expected to look forwards and backwards at the same time, to empower parents while holding the statutory authority. Even when workers train themselves to be virtuosi in the art of hat-changing, the results can be baffling for the client and undermining for the worker who is trying to use every ounce of effort to move forwards while having to watch out behind. It is to be hoped that one of the benefits of this book will be to encourage managers to think again about the way in which services are organised. However, for the present, workers in Britain will need to continue to develop their positional agility, holding both the child protection and the treatment roles continuously and simultaneously in their minds and perhaps discovering new and different applications for Insoo Kim Berg's ideas about the use of split messages.

Insoo Kim Berg's work will change practice and will open up new solutions for child protection workers who have become dissatisfied with a monitoring role and who are searching for ways to develop cooperation with their clients as a basis for building safety for children.

Evan George
Brief Therapy Practice
London, April 1991

One
WHAT IS FAMILY BASED SERVICE (FBS)?

GENERAL CONSIDERATIONS

Family Based Service (FBS) is a specialised service in child welfare that focuses on the family as the target of intervention, rather than on the child or the parents separately. It use the basic knowledge and skills developed in the field of family therapy to thoroughly assess and treat the family as a unit, usually in an intensive, time-limited period.

The philosophical underpinning and belief of the FBS program is that the best way to provide services to a child is through strengthening and empowering the family as a unit. Removing the child from the family is traumatic for the child and the family, no matter what the circumstances of the abuse or neglect. Many studies indicate that children placed in alternative care do not fare better than those children who remain with their parents over the long term. Therefore, it is believed that strengthening the existing parent-child bond and supporting the parents in doing a competent job is the best way to protect the children in the long run. Clinical experience often shows that even the badly abused and neglected child longs for his own parent and wants to go "home".

FBS is a sensible but drastic shift in the way we think about what is helpful for children and families. It requires specialised knowledge and skills to provide service to the family unit, the parent-child relationship, and other extended family and kinship relationships. FBS is designed to cooperate with the family by using the family's resources together with the formal and informal network of community resources.

By involving the family as a partner in the decision making and goal setting processes, and by recognising, respecting and using the family's existing strengths and resources, FBS strives to enhance the family's sense of competency and control over their own lives. The result is that families feel empowered and can become a safe and nurturing environment for the children while maintaining the unique cultural and other characteristics of each family unit. With such help, families are able to live independently with a minimum of outside interference.

HOW IS FBS DIFFERENT FROM OTHER SERVICES TO FAMILIES?

For a long time, the field of child welfare took an adversarial position with parents and frequently saw the children as the victims of bad or incompetent parenting. Often, the solution to a problem viewed this way was to separate the children from their parents, thus putting them in the hands of alternative programs, such as "foster care". The intent was to force the parents to learn to be better parents. This period of separation was thought of as a time when the parents learned new and better parenting skills so that when they were reunited with their children, the family would function better. In reality, these ideals were not achieved.

Parents were given conditions under which they would be allowed to reunite with their children, such as, getting a job, cleaning up their apartments, learning better parenting skills through attending classes, and engaging in counselling to solve the underlying problems that were thought to cause them to be abusive and neglectful of their children. They were expected to cooperate with social workers and follow their directions. Many parents did just that. Some reluctantly went along with these mandates and successfully reclaimed their children. However, most of these statutory clients got labelled as "unmotivated" or "resistive to therapy", as those who "minimised" or refused to "own up to" their problem.

Furthermore, such practices, based on simple "cause and effect" notions viewed from an individually oriented perspective, had the effect of creating more hardship and trauma for the children. Not only did the intention of rescuing the children from their bad parents result in punishment for the children, but it also became increasingly difficult to reunite the parents and children the longer they were separated.

Instead of encouraging cohesive and cooperative relationships as was intended, such practices had the effect of fragmenting the family and creating adversarial relationships amongst the family members. Communication became difficult amongst separate workers assigned to the child, the parent, and the foster parents. When legal issues surfaced, there were cases that had 3 different attorneys representing 3 different views of what might be good for the family. For example, I once worked with a family of 5 represented by 5 different attorneys: one for each parent because each had different goals, and one for each of the 3 children because all 3 were above the age of 12 and were entitled to individual legal representation.

In recent years, there has been an increasing awareness that the best way to help the children is to strengthen the family unit. Several factors led to this shift in thinking about the welfare of the children: a renewed recognition of the importance of the emotional bond between children and their parents, the fragmenting effect our child welfare policy has had on the family, and the recognition that a lot of money was spent with very few positive results. (Peter Forsyth, 1988.) Workers' efforts to transform such "involuntary" parents into cooperative, hard working, and motivated clients able to use individual treatment, support groups, and parenting education classes, has had a limited success.

Lack of success with these statutory clients is often blamed on the hostile and angry personality of the client, her* lack of education and intelligence, and the

* The client is referred to as "she" throughout since most clients tend to be single parent "mothers". The author recognises that many clients who are single parent "fathers" and the client is "the family unit". For identification, therefore, the worker is sometimes referred to as "he" although it is recognised that a large number of workers in this field are female. This in no way reflects sexual stereotyping.

impossible demands the system makes on the workers. All these are true. However, I contend that a more serious problem lies in the way we conceptualise the problem and thus arrive at solutions. The goal in child welfare must be to protect children through the strengthening of their families.

For too many years the goal of child welfare has been the "protection" of children. When the worker's goal is to "protect" a child, it implies that the child needs protection from someone, usually the parent. Thus, when a worker enters into a family system uninvited, takes on an investigative position on the side of the child against the parent, and starts to tell them what they must do, it naturally becomes an adversarial and hostile relationship. To add insult to injury, the parent is often treated as if guilty until proven innocent. No wonder the worker feels frustrated, stressed, and burned-out, and that this results in extremely high staff turn-over, as high as 50% in every 6 months in some agencies.

To return to the topic of the clients, these parents are often viewed as having defective and faulty notions of parenting, lacking problem solving skills, having no interest or ability to become good parents, and being full of psychopathologies. Filling such a bottomless pit of deficits and solving "multi-problem" cases is an exhaustive and thankless task for the worker if this is how he conceptualises his job.

I believe that it is possible to "treat" statutory cases successfully when the worker sets his sights on client strengths rather than on weaknesses, searches for exceptions to the problem, helps construct a different future through "miracle questions", and sets small and achievable goals. The premise of the Solution Focused Therapy model described here is that change is inevitable, not a hard-won commodity. In the following chapters, I will describe the role of the worker, the cornerstone of which is respect and admiration for the client's courage in struggling with the problems of living. This book will describe in detail how to establish a positive client-worker relationship, how to assess for change, how to ask questions that will generate solutions, and various techniques of intervention.

HOW IS FBS COMMONLY PRACTICED?

FBS (also called Home Based Treatment, Family Preservation, In Home Treatment) has the following characteristics:

1. The ultimate purpose is to provide services to the family as a collective unit with the goal of preserving the family, while insuring the safety of the family members.
2. The delivery of service is intense, immediate, and goal oriented.
3. Service is provided by a treatment team (often made up of case manager, worker/therapist, and support staff such as the home-maker, child care worker, and so on). Following a period of need assessment, clear treatment goals are set, well-laid out implementation plans and a termination plan are formulated. The client participates in each phase from beginning to end.
4. Each worker carries a limited number of cases for a designated period of time

(such as 90 days, 120 days, 6 months). Most treatment is offered at the client's home, although some programs have facilities for office visits.

5. Some programs combine a generic treatment service, with specialised services for cases involving, sexual abuse, alcohol and drug abuse, and domestic violence.
6. FBS is designed to respond to each individual family's unique needs. Therefore, the treatment approach is tailored to fit individual families.
7. Staffing is decided at intake and frequent case consultation occurs on an on-going basis.

ADVANTAGES

It is easy to see the advantages of the FBS program to both clients and workers. Lower case loads mean more intense contact with the client family, thus, more information is available to the workers. More frequent observation of the family's functioning gives workers more opportunity to intervene in a timely fashion. With the positive changes clients show, worker enthusiasm is high, clients do better, and cases get closed sooner.

The majority of protective cases start out as involuntary clients or clients who are afraid of having their children taken away. They not only need reassurance that the worker is interested in keeping the family together, but also that the worker's job is to offer them services that will strengthen family functioning. Clearly it takes skill and time to influence clients to move beyond their initial reluctance and fear. FBS has had more successes in this respect than traditional child welfare practices.

Working with multi-problem families in any setting can easily overwhelm the worker who is thus less effective than he or she could be. By identifying specific, concrete, measurable goals to work towards, and sometimes with time limitation, both the client and the worker can mobilise energy and resources, thus increasing the chances of success.

A team work approach supports the difficult decisions that workers must continually make. Much of the clinical aspect of child welfare work requires the worker to make judgments and to interpret data that is by its nature ambiguous. Having a team member who has another view or a different way of doing the same thing increases options as well as reassures the worker about safety issues. Having the opinion of another person on your side is simply more reassuring. The experience of many FBS teams across the country has shown that it reduces staff burn-out, and improves staff morale and enthusiasm for the work. It is not difficult to understand that the energy and excitement the worker feels about what he does can easily become contagious with the client.

DISADVANTAGES

The disadvantages of FBS include the requirement that the worker must think differently about his role, and conceptualise differently about the families he treats. Instead of being a broker who matches what the client needs with the resources in the community, the worker becomes the treatment person. Thus, it requires a new set of skills and new ways of doing things.

It requires the workers to respond immediately to the needs of the family, to show flexibility and the willingness to do things differently, and to be innovative and creative. It also requires workers to cooperate, become team members, and to take risks by exposing their work to colleagues.

Most of all, to be successful, FBS requires different organisational support and flexibility from management and supervisors who need to understand and support the FBS philosophy. Without system-wide support, backed by a willingness to reorganise the agency structure if necessary and on-going training, workers cannot carry out this difficult but rewarding task.

For the worker, it takes time and a shift in the way he approaches his work. He must recognise that the work he does right now may bring about a difference in the client's life some time in the future. Therefore, the worker must learn to be patient about the client in a different way. Other community systems, such as, the school, court, the medical system,and even other social service systems will require time to be educated about the unique and creative nature of FBS.

HOW HAS FBS BEEN INFLUENCED BY FAMILY THERAPY?

The basic concepts and philosophy of FBS are heavily influenced by Family Therapy. Family Therapy has developed over the past 40 years from a simple observation that an individual's behaviour happens within the context of an environment, that the environment influences this behaviour, and that, in turn, the environment is influenced by the individual's behaviour. Interactionally, since B is part of A's context, what A does influences what B does and B's reaction influences what A does.

This simple observation changed the location of the "problem" from being a) something that an individual has, to b) something that is part of an interactional system. By changing the boundary around the concept of "problem", family therapy also changed the boundary around the parallel concept of solution. That is, the family became both the unit of observation and the unit of treatment.

Family therapy is based on the idea that the family can be seen as if it were a rule governed system. For instance, an observer might notice that when A nags, he can predict with some certainty that B will withdraw. An observer might also note that when B withdraws, he can predict that A will nag. The observer might then say that A and B appear to follow this rule: if A nags, then B withdraws, and when B withdraws, A nags. Which comes first, nagging or withdrawing, depends on when the observer starts describing what he observes. With the enlarged boundary, the problem is not simply that "A is a nag" or "B is withdrawn". Rather the problem can be seen as involving the interaction between nagging and withdrawing.

Family therapy is based on the idea that human systems are fluid, evolving and changing, and that within this particular context there is no clear connection between "cause and effect". For instance, there is no way for either participants or observers to know whether A's nagging caused B to withdraw or, B's withdrawing caused A to nag.

Family therapists tend to believe that when there is a shift in the nature of interaction amongst family members, this will make it possible for the individual member to change; and when the individual member changes, the rest of the family will be affected in turn. The context or environment must also change to accommodate the individual's original change. That is, if A stops nagging, then B will change by either stopping withdrawing or withdrawing more. If B stops withdrawing, then A will change by either stopping nagging or nagging more. Either way, there will be some sort of change.

However, as we all know, stopping undesirable behaviour is not easy. A will find it far easier to substitute a different behaviour for the nagging than to simply stop nagging and B will find it easier to do something different rather than to stop withdrawing. Although A and B might not be able to see it, an observer will be likely to notice that there are times when A and B interact without either nagging or withdrawing and these non-nagging, non-withdrawing behaviours could be used to change the nag-withdraw pattern. For instance, any one of A's typical non-nagging behaviours toward B might be substituted for the nagging when B withdraws and then B will be likely to respond without further withdrawing.

The interrelationship between an individual and an environment led family therapy to the idea that a small change by A can be followed by disproportionately larger changes in A's family. For example, if A starts being nice to B and B responds positively, then this shift can create a chain reaction within their context. The more often A and B repeat this positive exchange, the more likely it is that this will influence C and D. This is called a "ripple effect".

With an enlarged boundary around solutions, family therapy points to the idea that developing solutions within the interactional context depends on at least one of the involved individuals doing something different from their predictable behaviours.

As you can easily see, this is a radical departure from the traditional assumptions about individual mental health problems and treatment. In this traditional view, the individual must get well before behaviours change whereas in the interactional view, the individual's behaviours may change as a response to changes taking place outside that person. It is easy to see that, compared to traditional individual psychology, this interactional view tends to be more optimistic about the potential for change.

This way of looking at the child and his social relationships has a significant impact on the way we provide child welfare services: instead of looking at the individual child or the parent as the focus of change, the individual child and the parents are looked upon as a resource for change.

The clinical practice of Family Therapy is significantly different from an individually oriented treatment model. Even when an individual client is treated, the therapist looks at her problems within the family context and looks at how she is influenced by and affects the rest of the family. Therefore, the treatment focus is on the family interaction patterns, and not on the individual psyche.

SOLUTION FOCUSED THERAPY

Solution Focused Therapy, a model of intervention developed and described by de Shazer (1985, 1988, 1991), Insoo Kim Berg (1988, 1990), and their colleagues at Brief Family Therapy Center in Milwaukee, is a new treatment model that is considerably different from others.

It is based on some of the same interactional, individual-in-the-context-of-the-environment ideas as family therapy. From that same philosophical base, it departs significantly in a number of different ways. The most important difference is the view of change. Unlike the accepted view of family therapy that the family unit operates on a principle of pressure to maintain a homeostatic balance and maintain its boundary, Solution Focused Therapy views change processes as inevitable and constantly occurring. Like the Buddhist view that stability is nothing but an illusion based on a memory of an instant, it views human life as a continuously changing process.

Taking this basic view, Solution Focused Therapy pays close attention to the exception to the problem, that is, when there is a small change to the stability of the problem state, and sees such exceptions as a key to finding solutions. It is easier to enlarge on the existing change, however small, than to create something that does not exist.

FOCUS ON SOLUTIONS, NOT ON PROBLEMS

Solution Focused Brief Therapists believe that it is easier and more profitable to construct solutions than to dissolve problems. Their clinical experience is that activities that center around finding solutions are distinctly different from problem solving activities. It is simpler for the client to repeat already successful behaviour patterns than it is to try to stop or change existing symptomatic or problematic behaviour. For example, the activities a worker may engage in to "protect a child" from his abusive or neglectful parent are quite different to those which the same worker would engage in when focussing on "building safety" for the same child. What the worker will do becomes even more different when he looks for and finds periods when the parent is already successful in insuring the safety of the child. This clearly is an easier and simpler type of solution.

Clinical activities that help to enlarge and enhance those behaviours around exceptions to the problem provide the keys to finding solutions. The following are important ways to look for exceptions.

PRE-SESSION CHANGE

Frequently, clinicians encounter clients who report that since they have been contacted by the child welfare department to set up an appointment for a home visit, things have changed markedly and in the direction they wanted their life to go. When the staff of Brief Family Therapy Center paid close attention to this phenomenon (Wiener-Davis, Gingerich, de Shazer, 1988), they found that about two-thirds of their outpatient clients report some form of positive change in the area in which they were seeking help through therapy. Understanding and paying attention to such pre-session change leads to quick solution finding since the initiative for positive change has already started to work and the family already knows what they need to do in order to bring about even a small change.

Unless they are asked, most clients often do not think a change is significant enough to report because it appears such a small change compared to the massive problems they are faced with. Most workers either ignore reported pre-contact change, or they brush it aside as a "resistive" maneuver or as "minimising" the seriousness of the problem.

Since the client has already made positive, goal-related changes, the worker's task is to amplify, reinforce, and help the client to repeat the positive changes they have already made on their own. Later chapters will describe the techniques for implementing this approach.

WHAT ARE EXCEPTIONS?

Exceptions are those periods when the expected problem does not occur, for example, when a child who "fights all the time" or "lies all the time" has a period when he is "cooperative" or "honest". When a great deal of attention is paid to the interactional patterns around those periods, that is, what mother does, how the child starts to be cooperative or honest, what else goes on when he "behaves", and so on, clues may be found as to what the client needs to "do more of". To most clients, at first, exceptions to the problem seem unimportant or insignificant. However, when both mother and son can find ways to repeat the behaviours that surround exceptions, the problematic situation becomes less overwhelming, more manageable, and eventually disappears.

Change occurs in many different ways: emotional, perceptual, and behavioural. When feelings towards a problematic situation change, it is possible to make a perceptual shift, followed by different behaviour; when a problematic situation is perceived as positive, one can make behavioural changes and think and feel differently about the same problem, thus creating different emotional reactions; when one behaves differently, emotional and perceptual changes follow. These are as interconnected and interrelated as A's nagging behaviours are related to B's withdrawing behaviour, making it difficult to figure out which came first, the familiar "chicken or egg" dilemma. Instead of trying to figure out whether it was the feelings, the thoughts, or the behaviours that came first, paying close attention to how the client made the shifts is much more profitable. Repeating these small but successful behaviours forms the basis for solutions. They become the keys and clues for solution. Details on how to tackle such trigger points are described below.

DELIBERATE AND RANDOM EXCEPTIONS

In our study of exceptions, we found that there are two types of exceptions that clients describe: deliberate and random.

A deliberate exception is one which the client is able to describe creating in a step-by-step fashion. An example of such an exception is: "I forced myself to get out of bed, forced myself to go downstairs, made coffee, got the kids off to school, and forced myself to get out of the house. It helped me to feel a little bit better about myself." Since the client can describe what she did, she can repeat those behaviours that helped her to feel better. Clearly the task for the client is to "do more of it".

Where random exceptions occur either the client is unable to describe her successes or she attributes them to someone or something as if she had no control over the episode. For example, the client will describe the day she felt a little less depressed as "I have no idea what made the difference on Wednesday. I just woke up feeling better", or "It was the day a package arrived from my grandmother who raised me", or "When I woke up the sun was shining and I felt better". Since the client sees herself as having had no part in creating the exception, it is difficult for the client to replicate. Such situations call for a different intervention or task, one of predicting what kind of day she will have the next day. A review the next day of what she did to have "a good day" and how this is different from what happens on "bad days" will provide directions on what to "do more of". More about this will follow later.

GOAL SETTING

FBS cases, more than any others, require clear goal setting if the worker is to avoid the dangers of interminable contact, possibly only terminated by emergency intervention to protect the children.

There are two different ways to negotiate goals. One is through setting a defined number of sessions, 5, 10, or 20 or by determining a period of time over which to meet, 30 days, 3 months, 6 months, or a year, and so on, marking the end of the contact through a lapse of time. Such an approach has positive and negative aspects. The positive aspect is that both parties will know clearly when the end of the contact will occur and work towards that date. The negative aspect is that both parties can just "buy time" waiting for the end to come, with no clear sense of what has been accomplished.

The second approach is the one I advocate: having clear, well-formed goals that can be described in a specific manner, and are concrete enough so that they become outward indications of the internal changes that are occurring.

The "Miracle question", a goal setting and solution finding technique, helps the client specify how things will be different once the problem is solved (see Chapter 6). Clients are asked the following question: "Suppose there is a miracle tonight while you are sleeping and the problem that brought you to the attention of child welfare is solved. Since you are sleeping, you do not know that a miracle has happened. What do you suppose you will notice that's different the next morning that will let you know that there has been a miracle overnight?" This "miracle picture" is used as a roadmap for figuring out where the client wants to get to and for suggesting what needs to be done to accomplish the desired changes.

The model described here is often characterised as "goal driven", that is, the therapeutic activities that both client and therapist engage in are always related to goals. Unlike the medical model, where the professional becomes an expert whose role lies in diagnosis, setting goals for the client and laying out the plans for the client to implement, Solution Focused Therapy follows the client's goals. For instance, when the client says to the worker her goal is to "get the social service out of my life", the worker agrees with the client that it is a worthy goal to work towards since the ultimate goal of the worker is to successfully terminate the contact with the client. When the goals are laid out by the client, not defined and imposed by the worker, the client is more likely to be committed to achieving them.

Guidelines for setting "workable" goals for FBS will be described in chapter 5.

THERAPIST ROLE

It is already clear that Solution Focused Therapy calls for drastically different activities on the part of the worker. The worker-client relationship is conceptualised as the product of the interaction between the worker and the client, thus forming a unique but temporary system engaged in finding solutions to the client's problem. When the task is accomplished, the relationship ends.

The worker is actively involved with the client in looking for pre-session change, exceptions to the problem, constructing imagined solutions, asking questions that will help the client to discover her own solutions. By asking what appears to be a simple question the worker is intervening in the system. Since the solution is generated from within the system it is more likely to be congruent because it is a natural part of the family system. Since the solutions are generated by the client and not introduced into the system from outside, the changes occur rapidly and the likelihood of setback is greatly reduced. Our study indicates that as time goes on, the "ripple effect" appears to create long-term positive influence. (Kaiser, 1988).

THREE RULES

1. If it ain't broke, don't fix it.

Simple observation will reveal that A and B are not always nagging-withdrawing-nagging. Even the most chronic of troublesome patterns is absent now and then. Sometimes, in fact, the problematic pattern is only a very small part of the client's life. Except in rare circumstances, even abusive parents do not abuse their children all the time. There are frequent periods, which sometimes last for a long stretch of time, when that same parent can be loving, quite nurturing, and behave in a very competent manner.

The concept of determining what is "not broke", and therefore, does not need fixing, is a subjective one at best, and not a scientific one. Workers need to have a very broad view of what "works" and "does not work" since much of what causes the client to come in contact with the child welfare services stems from extreme differences in culture and life-style.

2. Once you know what works, do more of it.

Solution Focused Therapists believe that paying close attention in detail to the period when the client is competent, nurturing, and responsible is much more productive since such positive behaviours form the basis for the strengthening of families. When each exception is studied carefully and who does what, when, where, and how is considered, it reveals a successful pattern. Since these are behaviours the client has already mastered, either recently or in past successes, it is fairly easy for the client to replicate those exceptions. Increasing the period of existing success is much easier than mastering new and different behaviours.

3. If it doesn't work, don't do it again; do something different

If one were to ask B "why do you withdraw?", chances are that he would tell us that he is trying to get A to stop nagging. As far as he can see, withdrawing or getting away is the only reasonable approach and he might say that he is convinced that he only needs to withdraw more or more effectively in order to get A to stop nagging. However, at least in a certain sense, B is accidentally reinforcing A's nagging. Although the folk adage of "if at first you don't succeed, try, try, again" might work in some situations, Solution Focused therapists will maintain instead "if it doesn't work, do something different." Thus, if B wants A to stop nagging, B might first notice times when A is not nagging him and notice what she is doing then. Then B should notice what he is doing when A is not nagging. For instance, B might notice that A never nags when he is holding her hand, or when they are talking in the kitchen. If B responds to A's nagging with his "normal" non-withdrawing behaviour, such as holding her hand, talking with her in the kitchen, then it is likely that A will cease nagging. In fact, the chances of A responding to B with her non-nagging behaviour will likely increase. Thus, A and B would have changed to the nag-withdrawal-hold-hands-kiss, more-talk-more-kiss sequence.

Two
THE INITIAL STAGE

WHAT ASSESSMENT IS DESIGNED TO DO

The most frequent misuse of what is commonly called "assessment" is when it is a laundry list of all the things that are wrong with the client. Therefore, you will often see a detailed account of what a poor childhood a client had, how she was abused, grew up in a foster home, has no contact with her mother, how she was "hooked up" with shady characters who used her, how each of her 4 children has a different father, and how she neglects and abuses her children now.

Such a list implies that the client is doomed to fail in life and, thus, even before the first visit, it is easy for the worker to take a negative view of the client. Such a view clearly will not help the client, especially since we all convey what we think and feel in subtle, non-verbal ways. Once we start to feel overwhelmed by the problems, we tend to look for ways to justify our failure, and so we describe clients as "unworkable", "unmotivated", "lacking insight", "resistive", "shopping around", or "not ready for therapy".

What is most important to remember is that the client may not agree with the laundry list of problems at all but may instead have her own ideas about what the problem is. If this is the situation, we have a clash over what the problem is and therefore over what to do about it. It is not hard to imagine how such clashes can lead to "client resistance", "avoidance", "passive-aggressive behaviours", or "non-compliance" from clients.

A way of avoiding such "resistive" or "uncooperative" client behaviours is to conduct an "assessment" in such a way that a list is made of activities that both worker and client need to do. Making a master plan to chip away the problems, aiming for small changes and making a list of activities that will move you towards the "easiest" way of finding solutions, will be a much more helpful way to "assess".

As you move along through this book, you need to bear in mind that the "assessment" is not best thought of as a list of "what's wrong with this client", but as a map which you and your client contract together in order to figure out where you both want to get to. Since you will be the guide, perhaps you need the map more than the client does.

A. PRE-ASSESSMENT INFORMATION

Before meeting with the client for the first time, gather all the data you have about the new case. It may be information from medical sources, court, school systems, relatives, church, neighbours, or from a previous contact with a protective service intake worker, the referral source, your supervisor or previous case worker

When you are reading the records from previous contacts, try to figure out what previous helpers have tried with this particular case, and also what they have suggested but obviously not tried. All the information about what not to do is contained in such records. Reading between the lines will give you some clues about how the previous worker and the client got along and even perhaps some ideas about how the previous helpers conducted themselves to get along with the client or how they failed. Obviously you do not want to repeat the previous helpers' mistakes and do more of the same things that did not work.

USING THE INFORMATION YOU HAVE ABOUT THE CASE

The following questions are useful to keep in mind as you sift through a lot of information you already have about a family that you have not even seen yet.

1. What mental picture do you have of the family?
2. What emerge as the strongest issues about the case?
3. What would the client see as the most important issue?
4. Who would be the most influential person in this family?
5. What is it that you should not do with this case?

Once you answer these questions in your mind, you will begin to draw a mental picture of the case you are about to encounter.

BEING OPEN TO CHANGE

Even if the client has been in treatment many times, it is always possible that the family's situation has changed since the last time. Sometimes, a new partner in the client's life, a new job, a new place to live, another child in the family, or a summer vacation from raising children alone, and so on, can make a world of difference in a positive way, but it can also create more stress in the family. It is very useful for the worker to be open to any possible changes, both good and bad.

It is best to assume that life is always changing and that each encounter with the treatment facility may be different. Be open minded and willing to see the client differently. Even for seasoned clients, and even if their life seems the same, contact with you this time is very different from their last contact since you will use a whole different treatment approach to child welfare: Family Based Services.

B. THE HOME VISIT
THINGS TO KEEP IN MIND

As you get ready for the session in client's home keep the following in mind.

1. It is an important part of your task to set the tone for a friendly, positive atmosphere in the client's home. Assume that you are accepted, be casual, and relaxed. The client is likely to take the cues from you.
2. Use your normal, everyday, conversational language, in a friendly, soft tone, using neutral words and phrases. If at all possible, use positive words. Instead of keeping hammering away about the "problems", use words like "troubles", "hassles" or "solutions". Imagine yourself talking to a neighbour over a cup of coffee around the kitchen table, whilst remembering that you are at work and

your conversation is a tool for change.

3. Learn to trust your own judgment and intuitive sense in your interactions with clients. As long as you maintain your respectful stance with the client, your ignorance at times can be turned into an asset for you.

4. Learn to use yourself as a tool for helping clients. Your common sense, observational skills and the way you use your senses will all become an important part of this use of yourself.

5. Always maintain a positive, hopeful view of the clients and your work with them. When you are hopeful about your clients, you tend to convey that to them in many subtle and non-verbal ways. Most clients are sensitive and intuitive about picking up cues from what you don't say as well as what you say. Learn about subtlety in interpersonal contacts and use it to help clients improve their lives as a result of their contacts with you.

6. It is essential that the worker pays attention to the parent(s) as well as to the children. Many parents are isolated, lonely, and can become easily threatened when the worker pays an inordinate amount of attention to the children.

7. When parents make many complaints about the children, it is a clue to you that you need to find ways to compliment their parenting. Most parents become easily threatened and defensive about their parenting, and tend to become harsher in their discipline. Defensive parents blame their children for bringing the workers into their home.

THINGS TO DO

There are positive and negative aspects to conducting a session in the home, and your skill is what turns the negatives into things that work for you.

1. Make an appointment for a visit. Ideally, ask for permission to enter the client's home as this will imply that you are willing to let the client invite you into her home. When invited, act like a guest, since that is what you are.

2. It is important that you should feel comfortable enough for your client to feel comfortable. Wearing "smart" clothes that may get soiled if the home is not clean will create a barrier between you and your client. When the sanitary condition of the flat is bad, you can comment on it by saying things like: "The landlord is not keeping up with his job of fixing things around here" or "The landlord should do a better job in keeping this place clean". These comments make a point without pointing the finger at the client.

3. Like a good guest, make a comment about something nice, attractive, or something they have clearly put a lot of effort into. Remember that a client's home is their personal space; you may not agree with her taste but it is important to respect it. Then ask which is her favourite chair and where she wants you to sit.

4. Make comments about the family photos, ask questions about who is who in the family. You may gain some important information through this.

5. Make the family members be experts on something you see in the home, such as, the pet, a woodworking project, knitting, puzzles, or accomplishments indicated by awards or plaques.
6. Schedule the home visits for a fixed time and day of the week. It provides some structure to a disorganised life.
7. Bear safety in mind, both yours and your client's. If you do not feel safe you will not relax and will not create rapport with your client. Do whatever you need to do to feel safe. You may have to raise the issue.
8. Distractions like the TV, telephone, children running around, dogs, neighbours or visitors coming in and out, can be a nuisance but you can also think of ways to use them. Do not hesitate to ask clients to lower the volume on the TV or the noise level in the home but phrase your request as one for help since you can get easily distracted.

    Example:

    "It would be very helpful for me and I would hear you better and give you full attention if you would turn down the volume a little bit." Or "I am having trouble concentrating. It would be very helpful if you could make the children speak in lower voices." Most clients are cooperative and willing to adapt.

The negative side of the home visit is clearly being in someone else's space or territory. Workers are not as familiar with "the lay of the land" as the client is, and have to adapt to the way clients do things, such as patterns of eating, standards of housekeeping, sanitary conditions, and so on. It simply calls for more flexibility of the worker.

C. THE CLIENT-WORKER RELATIONSHIP

It is, at times, very confusing to figure out who is most invested in change, who should be the main players in solving this particular family's problem. At times, the person who should be most concerned about solving the problem turns out to be the least bothered; instead someone else who the worker did not expect may be more willing to do something about finding solutions. Such confusion partly stems from the way we use the term "client" since it does not give us a clue as to who is most invested in working to solve the problem. In this section, I will describe some helpful ways of assessing worker-client relationships that will.

Not all worker-client relationships are the same, as most experienced workers know. Assessing what kind of relationship the worker has with each client helps him to know what to do, and what not to do in, order to enhance client cooperation and prevent worker frustration.

The worker-client relationship is never static; it is fluid, ever-changing, dynamic, and a back and forth interaction that changes over time, depending on why they are meeting over time. As you read this section, I suggest that you review some of the relationships you currently have with your clients and examine what type of relationships you have with them.

The worker-client relationship is the foundation for change. It is the basis on which the task of problem solving is built, but the relationship itself does not create change. Many beginner workers confuse this and expect dramatic change following a "heart to heart" talk when the client managed to "get it out" after years of "keeping it inside". It is a naive notion to expect that a change follows a discussion of one's feelings. It is just a beginning. Doing something about the problem is what creates change.

Many workers, counsellors, and therapists have found the following notions of assessing a professional relationship very useful. Keep in mind that these are not descriptions of the client, instead they form categories of client-worker relationships at a particular point in time, and the worker and the client share equally in forming these types of relationships.

THE VISITOR

The visitor-type relationship exists most often when the client is ordered to the worker by the court, job training programs, probation officer, school, family members, or by an employer. Such clients are thought to be resistive to acknowledging their problems or to be refusing to own up to the responsibility for the problems.

These are clients whose main goal is to avoid getting involved in the helping system, since from their point of view, there are no complaints or problems that they need help with. If they feel a problem exists, they think it to be of a nature that will not change, or, more frequently, they do not see the connection between their problem and any solutions the worker may offer. Their real goal is to end contact with the workers as soon as possible, and to be left alone.

If the client is reluctantly involved with the worker, it tends to be because of actual or perceived coercion. The reluctant or involuntary client will not take any steps to solve the problem the worker presents since she sees no reason for "being bothered". Frequently, a client may really see no connection between the predicament she is in and what the worker may offer.

The worker's task at this point is :
1. to "join" the client's world view as described in the case example below;
2. to find ways to influence, shape and mold the client so that she can identify problems and possible solutions to them. Once the client perceives that there is a problem, she can be engaged on a different level. This sometimes happens only after pressure from the Child Protection Services   "change things or you risk losing your children."
3. to agree, as far as possible, with the client's idea of what the problem is for her.

Clearly, some clients will take longer than others to progress, depending on the worker's skill in accomplishing the three tasks outlined above, and the client's experience with previous helpers. The more pressing the problem is to her, the more likely she is to take steps. The following is an example of how the worker "joins" the client, helping here to identify the problem and a possible solution.

Case example

Worker: Do you have some ideas about what we can do to be helpful to you so that your family can stay together?

Client: I keep telling you people over and over that somebody reported me when there was no reason to.

Worker: Do you have hunches or guesses about what he or she might think you need help with?

Client: Damned if I know. The police were here the other day because they thought the children were left alone. It's probably my mother who called. Well, she always meddles in my life just because I got pregnant when I was 17. She still thinks I'm 17 and treats me like it. She is convinced that as long as I keep my boyfriend, I will always be the worst mother in the world. I don't care what she thinks any more. Fred isn't going anywhere and you are not going to take my child and give him to her.

Worker: We don't want to do that and we don't want to keep coming here either. We have better things to do than to come and bug you. What do you suppose you can do so that your mother will not keep calling the Department and you will be left alone?

Client: There is nothing I can do. I've tried everything with that woman.

Worker: I am sure this is no fun for you. You have better things to do than have to put up with me coming here. Any idea about what you will have to do to keep your mother from bugging you like this?

Client: She wants to me get rid of Fred but as I told you it's not going to happen.

Worker: Obviously your mother is not convinced of how committed you are to Fred. Obviously she does not see the good things you see in Fred. What do you think will convince your mother that Fred is good for you?

Client: I guess I will have to let her come here more often and maybe not tell her about our fights. She thinks I am her baby and she has to protect me from Fred. He gets rough with me and the kids when he drinks.

Worker: You must love him very much. What do you suppose other people like your sister or your best friend would say is good for you?

Client: They think I shouldn't take all that crap from Fred. He gets me so mad sometimes, but he is a good father and he is good to me when he doesn't drink or use drugs. He goes to work every day.

Worker: So, what do you have to do so that you and Fred get along better and your mother will leave you alone and not call us?

Discussion:

The temptation for the worker is to jump in to a). rescue the client, as her mother repeatedly does and fails each time, or b) lecture her on what a bad influence it is to have Fred using drugs and alcohol. The worker wisely realised that if he were to take either step, he would only be doing "more of the same", and end up just as unsuccessful as her mother.

In contrast, by "joining" or siding with her, that is, acknowledging that she must have good reasons to stay with Fred in spite of everyone's advice to leave him, the worker focused on what the client needs to do. The worker not only avoided being dismissed as "just like everybody else", but also got the client to start thinking about what her responsibility is. This approach of asking questions is more likely to result in the client's own recognition that there is a serious problem between herself and Fred.

THE COMPLAINANT
This complaining-type of relationship is thought to exist when the client views her relationship with the worker as limited to providing information on the problems. The client does not yet see herself having a part in, nor is she committed to, taking steps to find a solution to the problem. However, the client usually perceives herself to be helpful to the worker by giving a detailed and accurate account of patterns, sequences, the historical narratives, speculations about the causes, and possible solutions that someone else might perform.

The client usually sees herself as an innocent by-stander or as having to endure the difficulties others inflict on her. Since she does not see herself as the cause of the problem, the client is likely to see the burden of solution lying with the person who she feels is responsible for causing the problem. For example, a mother with a badly behaved and uncontrollable child, or a woman in an abusive relationship may tell detailed stories of pain inflicted on her and even failed attempts to solve problems. The client sees herself as a victim of someone else's problems or even of bad luck. Having spent a great deal of energy and time trying to understand or speculate about the causes of her family member's problem, she sees the worker as allied with her. She may look to the worker to cure or fix the problem in the other person, to help to make her life less painful.

When the client is not yet at the point of seeing herself as involved in solution finding, the worker needs to be sympathetic to the client's predicament and thank the client for the helpful information she has provided. The worker needs to compliment the client on having the commitment to the family member that made it possible for her to "hang in there", and keep on trying to find a solution to a difficult situation.

It is easy to misread the complainant-type relationship as a customer-type. Remember that the level of distress the client feels or expresses is not sufficient indication that she is ready to take steps to solve problems.

The following conversation is an example of a worker with a complainant-type client.

Case example

Worker: What do you think will help you to get along with your daughter?

Client: I don't need no help. Lisa will have to get it into her head that she gotta behave or else I'm going to kick her butt.

Worker: Sounds like you have a big problem on your hands. So, what would it take for Lisa to start listening to you?

Client: That child will have to start listening to me and stop saying things like I beat her. I didn't threaten to kill her! She runs around and tells everybody I mistreat her. She lies and shop-lifts but everybody thinks she is a little angel and says it's all my fault. I didn't do anything wrong.

Worker: It's pretty tough raising a teenager alone. So, what do you think it will take for Lisa to start listening to you so that you don't have to get mad at her?

Discussion:

At times like this, when the client is not owning up to her problem but blames someone else or is seeing the solution as someone else having to change, but not her, it is too early to start talking to her about her part of the problem. The best thing to do is to take her side, be sympathetic, but stay focused on what she has to do differently to find the solution.

When faced with such clients, the most helpful thing the worker can do is to compliment the client for putting up with meeting him or following through referrals (if they actually do), or to comment on whatever positive things they are doing, such as going to work, sending the children to school, getting up in the morning, cleaning the house, keeping the children fed, showing up for a court hearing even though she sees it as being of no use to herself, or any small successes the client has made on her own.

Until the client has clearly indicated that she is ready to take steps to solve her problems, any suggestions the worker makes should be limited to activities involving thinking, analysing, or observing, and which relate to the complaint. Since the client is already doing many of these activities, she is likely to cooperate with the worker.

THE CUSTOMER

In the customer-type relationship both the client and the worker may not yet be very clear about the goals (see Chapter 5 on well-formed goals). However, in many ways, both verbally and non-verbally, the client indicates to the worker that she is committed to taking the necessary steps to solve problems, regardless of whether or not she believes she was responsible for the problem. Clearly not all FBS clients will be at this point when the worker gets started.

So, how can the worker tell that the client has the customer-type relationship with him? It is apparent when she says things such as "My life cannot go on like this anymore. Something has to change", "It's time I have to turn things around. But I can't do it alone. Can you help me?", "I tried everything to solve this problem. I don't know what else to do anymore. I need help", or "I will do anything to solve the problem. Just tell me what to do".

These are the clients who, for whatever reason, have reached the point of saying, verbally and non-verbally, that they are ready to do something to change their lives. Clients can reach this point by various routes, some good and some not so positive. When someone reaches this point, they can develop a fairly positive and cooperative working relationship with a worker.

Case example

Worker: What do you think it will take for you to have all these people out of your life?

Client: I have to get my act together; get rid of my boyfriend, concentrate on taking care of my kids, stay clean, take care of my business, keep going to CA meetings, and talk to people when I get upset.

Worker: What do you think it will take to stick with it? You said you don't handle boredom very well. You know taking care of the kids can get pretty boring at times. What do you need to do so that you can stick with it?

Client: I'm not sure but I have no choice. I can't ruin my kids' lives. They belong with me. I don't want no stranger to raise my kids.

Discussion:

Even when you have someone as motivated as this client, you need to stay focused on the goal by continually reminding the client about the goal and continually monitoring it.

D. WHAT TO DO IF OTHER SYSTEMS ARE INVOLVED

What other systems are involved in this case - the school, the visiting nurse, public health service, the court, another treatment person, the grandmother who raised the children and lives upstairs? As you identify the nature of the helping system involved in this case, doing and finding out the following things will be useful to you.

1. Make sure that you get that client's permission to talk to other sources because you don't want to duplicate services.
2. Make sure that you contact the person to let him/her know that you are working with the family.
3. Elicit that person's perception of the problem.
4. Find out who did what to solve what problem. Find out what worked and what did not work.
5. Figure out a cooperative way to work with him/her.
6. Find out what is the goal for the helping person?
7. Make sure that he/she is not more motivated to change the client than the client is to change herself.

Three
DEFINING THE PROBLEM

A. WHAT IS THE PROBLEM WITH THIS CASE?

Experienced workers know that there can be as many answers, if not more, to the question "What is the problem with this case?" as there are people involved. The problem as defined by the referring person, who may be a relative, neighbour, the police, school or public health department, may well differ from the client's definition of the problem, and may differ from your definition.

In negotiating the problem to be solved with the client, it is important, whenever possible, to stay close to the client's own definition since she is the one who will have to make the necessary changes. In addition, it is vital to negotiate a problem that can realistically be solved given the client's current situation and resources.

Asking yourself the following questions helps to organise your approach to the case in these early stages:

1. What is the referring person's view of what should be done with this family?
2. What is the client's view of what should be done?
3. What is your view? (or the team's, if you are a part of a team.)
4. If there is someone else playing a key part (e.g. Child Protection worker), what does he/she think needs to change with this case?

The following Case Example demonstrates the complexity of this process and the usefulness of addressing the questions suggested.

Case example

The school called the Protective Service, asking for an investigation into the possible neglect of 7-year-old Shranda. They reported what appeared to be a chronic state of neglect: poor hygiene and an unhealthy appearance; general changes in Shranda, who seemed withdrawn, listless, easily distracted, to be losing interest in her surroundings, and at times obviously hungry. They reported that the mother, Martha, did not respond to their letters and did not show up for conferences. Since there was no phone, they could not contact her.

The Protective Service report indicated a marginal level of neglect, nothing grossly abusive or neglectful, but certainly the family's functioning had been going downhill in recent months. Martha reported that she had been very depressed since she found out that she was pregnant again from her relationship with James. Her mother and sisters had repeatedly warned her against James who had recently been released from prison having served time for a terrible abuse of Martha. The pregnancy was the last straw and she now faced the difficult decision of what to do about it.

She agreed that things had not been going well for her and the children, and that she spent a great deal of time in bed, didn't prepare meals for them, and just didn't have the energy to do anything. Since there was no substantiated neglect, the case was referred for treatment at the community mental health center.

Since the client's view of the problem plays the most important part in forming the solution, the therapist spent a considerable time trying to establish what Martha's view of the situation was and what she wanted to do about it.

When sympathetically approached, Martha was finally able to agree with the school's concerns. She was a good mother once and she should have been doing a better job. Even though she had been reluctant to accept the outreach of the Protective Service and the school social worker initially, Martha was coming round to acknowledging that she had a problem, and that she needed help.

Discussion:

The teacher's initial concerns for Shranda had turned out to have much larger implications. Instead of being the simple marginal neglect case the school thought it was, the problem related to Martha's pregnancy, which had highlighted a strained relationship between Martha and her mother over Martha's relationship with James. Martha felt caught in the middle, being pulled from both directions, wanting to maintain both relationships, but realising that it was not possible. Clearly there was no simple solution.

The teacher, Martha, Martha's family and James might all answer the question "What is the problem here?" differently, and all these answers might differ from your answer. Having clarified the differences a further step needs to be taken.

B. WHO IS MOST CONCERNED ABOUT WHICH PROBLEM?

Assessing who is sufficiently concerned, upset or bothered to do something to solve the problem is vital. A number of common signs can help to make this distinction:

1. Strong emotions, both positive and negative, expressed as the problem is discussed.
2. Non-verbal cues that match the words of upset and concern.
3. "Something has to be done", "It can't go on any longer", "This is terrible", "Nothing I have tried works", "I don't know what to do any more" are some examples of the verbal content that typify an investment in change.
4. Obvious signs of emotional upset and stress are shown and some expression of a willingness to do something about it.
5. Expression of hopefulness about the situation, a belief that things could improve when the right context can be created.

The person who is most upset, is in discomfort, or indignant about the situation, is most likely to take some steps to solve the problem, and it is easier to follow where the energy is, than trying to create energy where there is none. If this person is in a position to take steps to solve the problem, then that is important to know.

If the assessment is that Martha's mother is most upset about Shranda not being taken care of properly, or Martha letting herself go, or James ruining her daughter's life, then it may be more productive to work with her mother than with Martha. If, on the other hand, your assessment is that Martha is most concerned about the state of her life, it may be more productive to work with Martha. If you are the person who is most concerned and upset, and most invested in change then it is clear that your client is a "visitor", not a "customer" for change, and needs to be treated as such until you see some change in her position. If you are the only person who is concerned and your concern is one of safety, then referral back to the Child Protective Service will be necessary.

C. WHAT ARE THE STRENGTHS IN THIS FAMILY?

It is easy to become overwhelmed by the extent, scope and the multiplicity of problems of the families that come in contact with the social services in general, and in particular the families with which FBS works. Frequently, these families are thought to lack even simple problem solving skills. When the worker believes this, it is easy for him to become overwhelmed and discouraged.

However, clinical experience of having worked with such families and the homeless (Berg and Hopwood, 1990) shows that clients are very resourceful and have enormous resilience. (Dugan and Cole, 1989) and strength. Their problem solving methods and techniques may be different from those of mainstream culture, but, by and large, they have solved many problems successfully. As indicated in Chapter 1, finding strengths and successes and enhancing and enlarging on them is the most productive and least exhausting way for the worker to proceed.

HISTORY OF PREVIOUS CONTACT WITH SOCIAL SERVICES

If there is a record on the file from a previous contact, even if it was not an intensive one, asking about it using neutral questions phrased in a casual way, may produce some useful clues about the client and her willingness to work with you.

Examples of useful questions at this stage may be:

"It seems as if the school is very concerned about your daughter and I understand that you have had some meetings with the school. How helpful were those meetings for you? What would you say the school did that was most helpful for you?"

"It seems like many people were concerned about your daughter. What do you suppose you did to get them to see that they didn't have to be worried?"

"The record indicates that you have had dealings with our department before. What do you suppose the worker did last time that was most helpful for you? (...least helpful?)"

"You have had some contact with the public health nurse before. Could you tell me what you found most helpful in your meetings?"

"You have 2 children in school. What do you think the school did that was most helpful for you and the children?"

Asking these questions will:

1. set you on the side of the client and thus put you in a position to evaluate her

previous contacts with helpers;

2. set you apart from but also give you some information about what was the client's view of her previous contact, and what she viewed as helpful or not helpful;
3. give clients the impression that you are trying to do what would be most helpful to them;
4. let the client know that you are willing to recognise her past successes.

If the client seems negative about her prior contact with professionals, refrain from defending the previous helpers and whenever possible, agree with the client - for the time being. It may be a difficult task but worth a try. Asking about the client's perception of her past successes in handling various "helpers" implies that you are aware that she was successful in the past.

FAMILY HISTORY: GENOGRAM

As we mentioned earlier, any "assessment" information must be useful in providing direction for what to do or where to go next. The "genogram" is no exception. Make sure it is clear that information from the genogram will be useful in relation to the client's and worker's goals.

What is a genogram and what does it do? It is an attempt to map out the family coalitions, alliances, historically significant events, life changing events, family myths and rules, and other significant issues that have had an impact on the client. Discovery of such events helps to place the current problems within the context of the family history and the social context of the family, thus giving the workers very useful clues to what might be the hidden issues.

The timing of asking for the historical information is crucial. Some clients may view it as being intrusive when they do not see how it relates to what they want from the worker at this time. On the other hand, talking about the family history can be a useful tool to help the client become curious about herself and her problems. Obviously you need to use your clinical judgment and common sense as regards timing. If you feel awkward initiating a discussion about family history or if the client acts as if it is strange, it is probably better to postpone going into it. Unless the discussion makes sense to clients, they are likely to see your attempt as irrelevant or intrusive and as such are unlikely to be stimulated to curiosity about themselves in a way that opens the possibility of new perceptions and change.

The genogram can reveal some important patterns in the family: the family myths that are both good and bad, the hidden ghost, the belief system about the clan, the family structure, who takes after whom, what shaped the client's view of herself, and so on. These patterns may have significant impact on the client's belief about her past and future. Family history can be a neutral, matter-of-fact issue or an emotionally charged one. You may need to gather information over several sessions, especially if the client seems reluctant to talk about her family. Reluctance could be an important clue as to what might be a sensitive issue. If so, do not force the issue before the client is ready to talk about it. During the assessment phase, the most important job is to motivate clients to do something about the situation that got them into contact with the helpers.

Remember, family history is a reflection of how the client sees her family, it is not always reliable or factual information, and it is negotiable. In retelling the story, clients modify, change, invent new myths, and drop some points. In other words, history is the client's construction, not made up of true or false statements, and with each retelling the story becomes more real. Accept the client's perception of her family. Elizabeth Stone (Stone, 1989) describes the wonderful ways people invent and re-invent family history. The worker therefore must be selective about the use of family history.

Many FBS clients have strained relationships with their family of origin, thus they may isolate themselves from a potential source of support. Frequently the client recognises that she was determined to be different from the way she was raised, but is upset at herself for doing the same thing her mother did. Find areas where the client has achieved a degree of autonomy and support the hard work it took to do it. When she feels successful, it is easier to be positive about her ties to the family of origin.

The following information should be obtained through a series of conversations, rather than by using a form. Encourage the client to elaborate on her view of the family, and make sure that your questions are phrased in such a way that the client does not answer "yes" or "no". Allow the client room to elaborate in her own words. You will not only learn the client's use of language but also her story of how she fits into the family.

1. What is the client's view of her family of origin?
The client may see her family (mother, father, siblings, grandmother, father, cousins, aunts, and so on) as a positive force in her life, a potential source of help, or a source of friction and a problem to be avoided. If her view is positive, the worker can emphasise this aspect and become curious about how she chose to adopt the positive traits of her family. If her view is negative, the worker can ask how she was smart enough to know how not to adopt those traits. The client can be asked how successful she feels she has been in what she set out to accomplish. Give the client credit for having achieved a degree of success.

Case example 1
Client: My parents always told me that I would never amount to anything. They never showed me affection, never kissed or hugged me. I guess my mother grew up in a family that didn't show any affection. She just didn't know how to help a child to have self-confidence. I believed for a long time that I would never be anything good. Then I started to rebel against that and told myself that I would show them who I really am. But then I did my rebelling by running away, getting pregnant, skipping school, getting into trouble with the law and stuff

like that.

Worker: So, how did you figure out that you were different from what they thought you were?

Client: I just knew it inside. I just wanted to prove to them that they were wrong about me and I was going to show them who I really was.

Worker: How did you do that?

Client: I wanted to be a good mother to my child, a better mother than the one I had.

Worker: Where did you learn to do that?

Client: I just watched other people do it and then imitated it.

Worker: That takes a lot of commitment to your child and also a brain to figure out what to do. How did you do that?

Client: I was going to be a different kind of mother. I swore that I would never make my child feel inferior and I never do. I never tell him he is a piece of shit.

Worker: You mean you had to teach yourself how to be a good mother? You must love your child very much.

Discussion:

When the client is successful in changing even a little bit of the family myth and making a positive move, for example, towards her image of what a good mother is, such departure from the family belief system needs to be supported and encouraged. It helps the client to know that it is positive to shape her own history in a way that is consistent with who she wants to be.

2. Where are the current alliances and resources?

Alliances amongst the family can be discovered by asking questions, such as, who visits whom and how often, who is the person that maintains contact with family members either by phone or letters, where does the family meet, who is the switchboard for gossip and information that gets passed among the family members, and whom does the client call when she needs help? Knowing this information will help the worker to know who might be the most influential person to involve in order to make changes.

It is useful to know, who amongst the relationships the client maintains in her family system has been most helpful to her and in what ways. It will help both the worker and the client to figure out what she does to maintain such a supportive relationship and what she needs to do more of to keep it. If she has lost some valuable support, what would it take for that family member to help her again? What are the rules for keeping the support and is it worth the emotional price she pays for it?

Example:

Worker: You mentioned that your grandmother has been an important source of help to you in the past. What do you suppose it would take for her to help you again?

Client: I suppose she would say I have to cut off James for good this time and not take him back.

Worker: That sounds like a tough choice. So, how will you know which is more important to you, keeping James or keeping your ties to your grandmother?

Client: It is tough to decide. I want my grandmother to be proud of me and to see my kids. They need that. I'm not sure about James. He has not been good for my kids. They are afraid of him and they shouldn't be. I don't know which is good for me, it's hard to decide. I guess I want both but I can't have both.

Worker: It sure is tough to decide. Is there some way you can have both?

Client: I'm not sure. I've never thought about that.

3. What is her family's view of her relationships with men?

This seems to be the most frequent source of conflict for FBS clients. The major reason for emotional cut-off and tension between a young woman and her family is the issue of the men she chooses. Therefore, important questions to ask when dealing with such women are: does the family approve of her choice of men; do they think she has done well with men over the years; what do they think she needs to do; what do they believe is the reason why she is attracted to men who they believe mistreat her? If her family is angry at her choice of men, obviously it is because they care about her intensely.

Case example

Worker: What do you suppose your mother would say she wants you to do about your boyfriend?

Client: She thinks all men use me, that I don't know my own mind and she's always telling me what to do. It really bugs me that she thinks I am so stupid. She never really let me choose my own friends, just because I made a mistake when I was 17.

Worker: What do you suppose will convince her that she does not have to worry about you now?

Client: Nothing will. Any guy I have, she always finds something wrong with. She is never satisfied. She didn't do so well herself, married to a drunk. She has such a boring life that I think she lives her life through me. I keep telling her that I am not going to live my life for her and then we get into big fights. That's when she calls the social service.

Worker: What small things do you suppose she has to see you do, for her to believe that you can take care of yourself?

Client: If I don't ask for money from her. If I manage my money, I suppose. She thinks I give my money to my boyfriend so that he can buy his booze.

Worker: Suppose you did not ask for money from her. How do you suppose she would react differently with you?

Client: She might nag a little less.

Worker: What difference would it make for you if she nags a little less?

Client: Then, I could enjoy talking to her. I don't want to cut off the apron strings altogether. I just want some room to be my own person.

Worker: How will you know you have become your own person?

Discussion:

Even when there appears to be an overwhelming conflict that dates back to the client's adolescence, with the worker's help it is possible for the client to begin to figure out what she has to do to achieve her goal in a constructive way, and to stop blindly rebelling against anything her mother advocates.

4. How great is the client's sense of autonomy?

Does the client think she has done well as a parent, a daughter, a professional, or as a person? For example, does she believe she has done a better or a worse job of parenting her child than her mother had done with her? What kind of parent does she want to be? How is she similar or different as a person from her mother? Information on these questions will give you a good sense of the degree of autonomy and separation between generations. The worker needs to pay attention to the smallest indication of independence and autonomy and to enlarge it.

Case example

Worker: You mentioned that it is important for you to be a different kind of mother than your mother was for you. How did you figure that out?

Client: I remember when I was a child I used to think how I will never be like my mother. I will never hit my own child, I will always listen to her, praise her, respect her wishes, and spend time with her and things like that to let her know that she is important to me.

Worker: How successful would you say you have been?

Client: I am still learning and I have a long way to go.

Worker: What do you suppose your mother would say about the kind of mother you are to your child?

Client: She would say I am doing a pretty good job.

Worker: How do you explain that?

Client: I worked very hard. I go to classes, I read a lot, I watch other people who I think are good parents and listen to them. Mainly I would say I listen to others.

Discussion:

This client clearly needs a lot of compliments for the intelligence and thoughtfulness behind her degree of success. Whenever the client breaks the family pattern, even to a small measure, by having made a conscious effort to change her behaviour and increase her sense of independence, such endeavour needs to be supported and credit needs to be given for the hard work it takes to achieve it.

If she thinks she has done a better job than her mother had done with her, how did she learn to do that? Has she taught herself or did she learn from someone else? Who did she learn from? Either answer could be an opportunity to compliment her - for having given a lot of thought to the issue, which is a sign that she cares about her children, or, for having had enough intelligence to figure out what she had to do to learn to be a good parent. If there was a critical event that changed her life, such as an illness, an accident, a confrontation, reading a magazine article or a book, attending a lecture on parenting, and so on, ask in detail about how she took advantage of such events to benefit herself

Information gained from the above questions will give you a global picture of what might be the family system-wide problems and also what potential resources the client can draw on. It also gives the worker ideas on what might be the general direction in which to move, whether to bring in the family members to the sessions or not. If the client sees her family relationship as negative, you may want to put off meeting her family until the client indicates that she is ready to do so. There is further discussion about how to make use of answers to these questions in Chapter 6.

Four
DEVELOPING COOPERATION

A. JOINING ACTIVITIES

Most therapeutic models and treatment approaches emphasise the importance of the client-therapist relationship and see it as the essential ingredient of any professional relationship. Obviously, when the relationship is positive, everybody tends to see things in a more positive way, and it therefore enhances the chances of positive results in this joint effort between client and therapist.

However, the client-therapist relationship should be viewed as a means to an end, rather than an end in itself. Whereas a positive working relationship enhances client motivation and helps clients to be more cooperative and open with the therapist, it would be a mistake to believe that in itself it is enough to change client behaviour. For that to happen the client needs to make a perceptual and cognitive shift, and to do something that is behaviourally different from what she has already been doing.

WHAT IS "JOINING"?

"Joining" is a term borrowed from family therapy literature, which we will use here to describe what the therapist needs to do in the engagement phase in order to establish a positive working relationship. It is primarily the therapist's task to reach out to the client, project a warm and positive feeling, and give the client confidence in the therapist as someone worthy of her trust. It is done through a variety of verbal and non-verbal, subtle and not so subtle, cues and activities.

The ultimate goal of "joining" the client is to make your job easier. When clients believe you are interested in them and want to work with them they are more likely to cooperate and work with you and to make changes. The ultimate beneficiary of your "joining" with the client is the client herself.

HOW CAN THE THERAPIST "JOIN" THE CLIENT?

1. Before meeting the client for the first time, put yourself in her position and imagine what you would want the therapist to do for you. Remember to set aside your personal feelings about the client and take a detached but curious stance with her.

2. Avoid professional jargon. Use simple, everyday language. Avoid bureaucratic or inflammatory words like, "individual", "residence", "level of education", "status", "perceive", "evidence", "abuse", "report", "investigation", "accusation", "allegation", "perpetrator", and so on. These are best saved for talking to your colleagues or supervisors and other professionals.

3. The first meeting sets the tone for positive contacts later on. You need to use friendly, positive words. Give some thought to what kinds of things the client

would be defensive about and make sure that you handle those carefully. Say things like, "My job is to keep the peace in the family. It is obvious that your family is going through some tough times and I wonder how I can help."

4. Look for key words or idiosyncratic ways the client uses certain words, such as "fussing", "bothering", "discussion" vs "argument", that seem to stand out, and try to mimic their use. For example, if a client says that the kids' "fussing" bothers her the most, you can incorporate her words by asking, "So when your kids fuss, what have you tried that worked?"

5. Behave as though you accept their way of doing, seeing and explaining things: even though it may not seem logical or realistic to you, it does to them.

6. Do not confront directly or do things that will make the client defensive. Always avoid getting into debates or arguments with clients. It works better when you take a "one down" position and say you are "confused" or "don't quite understand", and ask for further clarification. Most of us, and clients are no exception, like to help others and want to show how much we know.

7 Let the client be the "expert" on her problem and circumstances. As far as possible, do not tell her what her "problem" is. If you do that, and the client disagrees with that view, the burden of proof is on you, rather than on the client. This is a position that the therapist should not be in since it makes it easy for the therapist to become more of a "customer" than the client, and thus end up working harder than the client to solve the problem.

8. Instead of expecting the client to accommodate your way of thinking and doing things, remind yourself to adapt to her way of thinking and doing things. It makes things a lot smoother and will be less work for you in the long run.

9. During the early phase of your work frequently compliment your client on anything positive she is doing.

10. When treating the family, do not take the child's side but support what the parents are trying to do with their child.

11. Talk in a way that the client can relate to. If you have someone who is very concrete and has a low ability to abstract, you need to talk about what is important to her in a very concrete manner. If you have someone who is visually oriented, use visual words, such as, "So, what do you need to see different in your life that will tell you that things are getting better?" If your client uses auditory cues, use words like "so what changes will you listen out for that will make you tell yourself that things are better?" Someone who is kinesthetic will use many words related to feelings or actions. Respond in kind by saying, "So when you feel better about yourself, what will you be doing that's different from what you are doing now?"

12. Answer the following questions for yourself as you collect information.
    a) What is important to this client?
    b) What would make sense to her?
    c) What are her problem solving strategies?

d) What are her successes and failures around this problem?

e) How does she see the problem? How does she explain that she has this problem?

f) What is she willing to do and what will she not do?

g) What resources are there to draw on - the extended family, neighbour, church, special friend?

The answers to these questions will give you some ideas on how to adapt yourself to your client. When the client thinks you respect and validate her ideas, she will respect and validate your input.

Clearly, your job does not end with "joining". When you feel that the client is beginning to give you credibility, then your job is to influence the client in such a way that she does what is good for her.

Case example 1

The adoptive parents of an 8-year-old were extremely angry at the school for having paid attention to a fabrication which their child told his teacher about how he was beaten, given no food and tied to the bed. Apparently the school promptly called the Protective Service, the parents were "investigated" and the case was referred for counselling on their "family problem".

The parents were indignant at the school for having reported them, at Protective Service for coming out, and for having been referred for treatment, which implied that they were doing something wrong. They had adopted a child with many emotional problems caused by 8 different foster placements by the time he was 7 years old. Their lofty and loving intentions were causing them havoc in their lives, instead of the blissful family life they had imagined. They were angry about having to be there when they felt the real problem was the school taking the side of the 8-year-old.

Obviously these parents needed to be complimented for having taken on the tough job of parenting such a difficult child. What's more, even though they felt that they were "unfairly treated by the system" they were still willing to come to therapy and try to solve this problem once and for all. When the therapist was sympathetic to their plight, they relaxed considerably and became much less defensive.

Case example 2

The parents of a 15-year-old girl disagreed over discipline issues and threatened each other with divorce over their disagreement. It was related that their 15-year-old was "seeing" a 26-year-old man every day, going to his house, eating dinner there, and was on the phone to him all the time. Apparently the disagreement was related to whether seeing this man was good or bad for their daughter. Mother said, as did the daughter, that it was better than having her run wild in the streets, while the father had "no use for him" and at times was "ready to kill the guy". They said they needed help in deciding what to do.

The parents were complimented on agreeing to take steps, such as coming to therapy, and making sure that they did the right thing for their daughter. The therapist told them that she could see they loved their daughter very much and that they both had good points.

B. DEALING WITH RESISTANCE

WHAT IS RESISTANCE?

Many types of clients have a reputation for being "resistive". Examples are: teenagers, alcohol and drug abusers, statutory cases, school or social service cases, or clients who come to treatment under coercion by their family or spouse. They are thought to wilfully refuse to cooperate with the agency, to be sneaky, evasive, and often angry and hostile towards social workers and other helpers. There is a lot of "evidence" and experience that give weight to such bad reputations. Some clients are indeed unfriendly, reluctant to give information, and at times downright nasty, hostile, and threatening towards therapists. What do you do when faced with such a situation?

Since we have taken a systemic view consistently throughout this book, we need to apply the same concept to this situation as well. When looked at from the wider, systemic point of view, rather than seeing the "resistive client" against the "impartial, objective social worker", we can more helpfully see such "resistance" as a clash of cultures that often occurs when very different systems with opposing goals and expectations meet. What makes it worse is that the large system (such as the legal, medical, or social services) representing the community, often "barges in" uninvited and threatens the very survival of the other smaller system by telling them what to do, what they are doing wrong, and demanding that the small system change their views and values.

The belief systems, values, and priorities of the community agencies (mental health clinics, psychiatric facilities, hospitals, the schools, and so on), are very different from those of the client system. No wonder there is a huge gap. It is like the meeting of two different worlds, and this is literally true, more often than we would like it to be.

When cultures, values and goals clash, each side believes that the way they have always done things has worked for them, and therefore, not only is there no need to change their ways but everyone should adopt the same belief system; "it worked for me, and therefore, it should work for you, too." Of course the client system believes that theirs is the better way, unless they decide that changing is in their best interest. We see a small example of this in what happens between schools and parents: school blames the parent while the parent blames the school for the child's poor performance. Even though we as therapists do not like the idea, the community often uses the treatment system to enforce the community's values and as a tool for social control.

Essentially, family or client resistance is strongest when the larger system tells the smaller system what they are doing wrong and demands that they adopt different ways of doing things, when the small system has not invited or requested the intervention and fails to see the value of such changes.

Therefore, the burden of building cooperation between the worker and the client lies with the worker rather than the client. The worker's task is to build cooperation where there is very little and increase effectiveness against all odds. You can see why it is a big task, but it is one that can be rewarding in the end, as you will find out when you use the outline and techniques described in this book.

WAYS TO BUILD COOPERATION, NOT RESISTANCE

1. Have an open mind about the client and be prepared to give her "the benefit of the doubt."
2. Put yourself in her shoes and look at everything from that point of view.
3. Figure out what is important to your client at this time and see this view as a valuable asset that served her well over the years, although this very point of view may get her into trouble now and then. Maybe when she recognises that, she will be more willing to change.
4. Do not argue or debate with the client. You are not likely to change her mind through reasoning. If that was going to work, it would have worked by now.
5. Check once more how realistic your expectations for the client are, given her limitations and circumstances at this time. You may change your views later on, as will the client.
6. Look for the client's past successes, however small, ordinary, or insignificant. Ask how she achieved them. This question alone becomes a subtle compliment.
7. Look for any small current successes and ask how she accomplishes them and what it would take her to repeat or expand these into other parts of her life. It indicates your confidence in her ability to solve problems.
8. Look for positive motivation behind the client's behaviour and comment on it. She will begin to believe it herself.
9. If you have to choose sides between the client and another social service system, choose to be on the client's side until proven wrong.
10. Be willing to apologise to the client for any mistake or misunderstanding. It takes strength, self-confidence, and professional integrity to be willing to apologise, but, paradoxically, it gives you power in the relationship.
11. If a client is not home or is unavailable for meetings it may not necessarily be a sign of resistance. For many families, being on time is not an important factor in life.
12. Always use a gentle and soft voice, use positive, not negative words and non-threatening gestures.

13. Most clients respond better when you provide services that are related to immediate problems, such as, housing, food, diapers, day care, and so on.

MANAGEMENT OF ANGRY AND HOSTILE CLIENTS

This section will discuss some useful and successful strategies and techniques that will help you manage when faced with some unexpectedly hostile and angry clients. Some workers find this aspect of their work most the most stressful and difficult to manage. It is not only normal to become fearful of angry and hostile clients but it also alerts the worker to a potentially dangerous situation.

Since most clients are "referred" by other programs, such as the Child Protective Service, Alternate Care Programs, 24-hour workers, court orders, or at the recommendation of other programs and workers, they are supposedly "voluntary" to the FBS program. However, such cases of "voluntary participation" tend to have coercive elements.

Therefore, you may run into some clients who are openly angry and hostile towards workers, even though they may have agreed to participate initially. In most situations, clients are openly angry or hostile are easier to deal with and manage than those who adopt a passive-aggressive stance which is difficult to identify and resolve.

The client's anger and hostility can be attributed to the frustrating circumstances she is in, a chemically induced altered state, or extreme paranoia due to mental illness. Since this book is limited to FBS, we will address only those situations that can be managed by treatment approaches, and not those requiring force or other legal means.

Obviously you want to make sure that your safety is assured by doing everything you can to protect yourself when you have a prior warning about the level of hostility of the client or past history of violence. Since I assume that you are familiar with various techniques of defusing emotions, hostility, and violence, you are advised to refer to them. If it is known that some client has been hostile to other workers, ask previous workers or their supervisors what has helped to defuse the situation. You may want to try the same. Find out also what the other worker tried that didn't work.

Since you are interested in turning the difficult situation into one that is helpful to the client, always look for ways to use the situation to help the client feel more comfortable, empowered, and in control of herself.

WHAT TO DO WITH ANGRY AND HOSTILE CLIENTS

1. Normalise their anger and hostility towards you

   Allow your client to vent her anger and frustration for a few minutes. There is no need to defend yourself or the Department but listen quietly, seriously and with real curiosity. It is important to know your client's complaints.

   Accept her anger as perfectly normal and as making sense. Make it clear that you don't blame her for getting angry. In fact, you are surprised that she is not more angry at all those people coming and going in her life.

2. When the client seems to be calming down somewhat, start with a soft, quiet, almost mumbling voice, and indicate your admiration for her fierce independence and her desire to protect her privacy. It is an indication of her desire to run her own life and you absolutely agree with her wish not to be told what to do. Then, casually ask if she has always been such an independent person or is this something new for her? And by the way, where did she learn to be such an feisty, independently minded person? As you are saying this, make sure that you are not being sarcastic - you really must believe what you are saying. This is called "reframing", a term borrowed from family therapy literature (more about this technique later). Sit back and watch your client calm down and start to cooperate with you.

3. Next quietly ask her in what way can the worker or the FBS program help her remain independent and protect her privacy since it is exactly what you want for the client. For example: "So what would it take you to keep your privacy?" or "Absolutely, I agree with you. So, what do you have to do so that they will leave you alone to run your own life?" Do not get bogged down with the complaints and, after a brief period of venting, move on.

4. Distancing yourself from their target of anger
   Since you are agreeing with the client's perceived cause of anger, make sure that you do not identify yourself with their target of anger. For example, if the client is angry at the Children's Hospital for having reported her for a suspicious injury her child sustained, do not identify with the hospital or the doctor but distance yourself by referring to them as "they" or "the doctor at the hospital", and so on. This gives you some room to maneuver later on.

5. Give the person space to move around. Allow the client to leave the room or walk out of the house; meet in a larger room of the house.

6. Do not feel compelled to stay in a potentially violent situation. Allow yourself easy access to an exit.

WHEN NOTHING WORKS WITH THIS FAMILY

Even when the worker makes all the right moves with proper attitudes, and does everything right, it is still possible that you will not succeed in getting all clients to be cooperative. The reality is that there are limits to what the worker can do to influence the client. "You can draw the horse to river, but you cannot make it drink" is a good proverb to remember. Occasional failures to "reach the client" and establish a positive relationship reminds us that we must learn to accept our limitations. An important point to keep in mind is that the client has a right to self-determination and to accept the consequences.

C EMPOWERING CLIENTS

The "Mary Ellen" case of the 19th century, which initiated the child welfare movement in the U. S., was based on the notion of "protecting" the child from those around her who "abused and neglected" her. Therefore, it is logical that the child welfare policies and the workers who implement these policies tend to view their primary responsibility as "protection of the children". Clearly many child welfare programs are designed to do just that and there is a clear need for them.

WHAT IS "EMPOWERMENT" OF THE CLIENT?

The notion of "empowerment" of the client almost seems to be a new slogan taken on by the FBS field in recent years. Therefore, it may be useful to review this notion and how it is practiced in FBS.

Empowerment of the client is an idea based on certain philosophical views of human problems and their solutions. The treatment model described here empowers the client and is based on the notion that she is competent to make choices that are good for her. As stated elsewhere, empowering the client is not the same as condoning anti-social, illegal, or unhealthy belief systems or behaviours. Neither is it the same as "enabling", which has developed negative connotations in recent years through its association with the drug and alcohol treatment field.

The practice of empowering has the following features.

1. The basic belief about the client-worker relationship is that it is a collaborative joint venture between the client and the worker.
2. It is assumed that the client is competent to know what is good for her and her family.
3. It is further assumed that the client has the ability to solve problems and has solved problems in the past.
4. The client determines and negotiates the goals for the contact.
5. The client participates in the treatment procedures and selection of options that are suitable for her since she is assumed to be the expert on what is good for herself, her life, her body, and her family.
6. The technique of complimenting the client is an expression of these assumptions about the client.
7. The emphasis on exceptions to the problem assumes that the client does solve problems on her own. Interviews are designed to uncover such solutions and successes.
8. The client is in charge of the termination of contacts.
9. It is an approach that respects client autonomy and personal, familial, and cultural boundaries, and is thus less intrusive.

The most important thing to keep in mind is the concept that clients need to feel in control of their lives as much as possible. Client participation in goal setting and solution finding allows them a voice in determining the course of their lives. This is a very respectful way to work with clients, rather than for them.

The more success they have, the better they will feel about themselves. Here follows an example of empowerment in action.

Case example

A single mother had a lot of difficulty controlling her children. She came to the attention of FBS because one of her children was molested by a baby-sitter. The mother had felt criticised by various helping professionals for not being consistent and not being able to follow through with the rules she set. She was constantly overwhelmed by the children's problems: failing in school, behaviour problems, and a chaotic home situation. She was always tired and under stress. The children needed protection from her ex-husband who in the past had been physically abusive of her and the children, and was suspected of sexually abusing a daughter, yet she felt helpless to do anything. The children were out of control and needed structure, consistent discipline, and follow-through to provide them with a sense of security.

By chance, the FBS team found that she was amazingly successful as a supervisor of the housekeeping department of a large motel chain. She received frequent promotions because she was effective as a supervisor, she loved her work, and was clearly good at it.

Based on the empowerment philosophy, the team decided to explore the idea that her ability to supervise could be translated into being a mother. The team decided to help her see herself as a supervisor of her children. Effective supervision of children requires basically similar skills and approaches to those involved on her job. The result was very positive.

In this example, the first task of the worker was to start seeing this mother as a competent, effective person and to start looking for her strengths. The imagined solution the team came up for this family was for the mother to start to "supervise" the children with clear rules and expectations, and consistently follow through by praising, setting limits, frequent evaluations, rewards and punishments. All of these techniques she was already using effectively. The team discovered that in her mind, "parenting" was something entirely different from "supervising". Therefore, the team kept referring to her task in the home as the "supervision" and "management" of her children. It appeared with this mother there was an emotional block to the word "parenting".

Five
SETTING GOALS AND CONTRACTS

Unclear goals invariably lead to a long-term contact. They also cause the worker and the client to become easily frustrated with each other, which frequently ends in mutual blame. Of the hundreds of cases I have been consulted on, supervised, and taught about around the world, the most common reason for therapists, counsellors, and social workers to feel "stuck" is related to unclear goals.

Negotiation of contracts for meetings between the worker and client and goal setting starts as soon as the client comes into contact with the social services. At the time of the very first contact with a family, the Child Protective Service intake worker must be clear about what the purpose of his first home visit is, whether it is to be an investigative or a therapeutic one. Although it seems obvious at first, it can easily be confusing. For example, only about 30% of the cases where there has been a complaint against a family actually turn out to have some basis for further investigation. This means that the other 70% of cases are potential treatment cases and the worker must be clear about his goal in each of these cases, re-contracting with the client on a new voluntary basis.

From the beginning of contact with a family through to termination, the worker must keep a steady eye on the goals negotiated with the client. This chapter will deal with contract negotiation, guidelines for setting goals, goal maintenance, re-negotiation of goals, and on-going evaluation of treatment goals.

A. NEGOTIATION OF TREATMENT CONTRACTS

As most FBS workers know, not all clients who come into contact with the FBS programs are "voluntary" clients. However, even the "involuntary" clients have a voluntary aspect to their contacts with the worker. Even the clients who meet with the worker because of the court order did not really have to do so. They had the option of taking the consequences of refusing to meet with the worker. It is useful to keep in mind this "voluntary" aspect of the "involuntary" client.

Negotiating treatment contracts with clients who want the worker to stay out of their lives is very difficult at first, but not impossible. When handled skillfully, they can turn into hard-working clients, and can succeed in achieving their goal of keeping the FBS workers out of their lives.

Before you start the negotiation of goals, refer back to the description of "involuntary" clients who are "visitors", and ways to work with them. Again, keep in mind where the client "is", that is, if their goal is to "stay out of the District Attorney's office" or to "get the social worker off my back", or to get "my parents off my back", that is a perfectly reasonable goal. In order to achieve such goals, the client will have to make certain changes, such as getting up in the morning, going to work or school, coming home on time, and so on, which are good for her.

The following gives examples of the questions that can be used in the beginning phase of the contract negotiation.

Worker: I know that coming here is not your idea of how to spend an evening. Any ideas of what you would like to get out of coming here that will make it worthwhile for you?

Client: It was very hard for me to make the phone call. I was wondering on the way over here what I would have to tell you. I think I need help. My life is a mess.

Worker: Yes, I am sure it was very difficult for you to come here.

Client: Well, I don't know. I don't want people messing with my life.

Worker: You know, Anita, that's exactly what we want. We want to get out of your life as soon as possible. What do you suppose you have to do so that we stay out of your life and leave you alone? What did Mrs. K. tell you about that? We are wondering how badly you want to keep your children with you.

Client: Real bad. I'm their mother and kids should live with their mother.

Worker: We absolutely agree. We know that you love your children more than anybody, and that you know what is best for them. So, how badly do you think you want to change things so that they can continue to live with you?

Discussion:

In this exchange between the worker and the client, the worker sets a positive tone by assuming that the client wants the children with her and explaining that he wants the same thing. Having thus put himself on the client's side, the worker proceeds to negotiate what the client wants to do to achieve her goal of keeping the children together.

Taking a sympathetic stance with the client does not mean we condone the client's abusive or neglectful behaviour; it only means that the worker is open minded and that the client will get a fair hearing. This approach makes the client less defensive and allows her to be more open and honest with the worker. Clearly the client will test the worker to find out how much she can really trust him, given all the bad stories she may have heard about Child Protection Service and social workers in general.

B. GUIDELINES FOR GOAL SETTING

The professional worker-client relationship is a purposeful one, that is, it is designed to achieve certain goals. Its success or failure will depend largely on what kind of goal you agree on and what methods you use to achieve the goals. If you do not have clear goals, neither of you will know when you have succeeded and it will be difficult to evaluate the work you and your client are accomplishing.

Goals have two components: what you are aiming for and how and what you are going to do to achieve it. The following are important guidelines for setting workable goals. When these guidelines are followed, you are likely to find that you will enjoy your work.

1. The goal must be small, simple, and realistically achievable

Sometimes big problems can be solved with small, simple solutions. We frequently overlook the most obvious ones, thus, complicating the problem solving activities unnecessarily. It is obvious that the goals you help the client negotiate should be something the client can realistically do, given her circumstances. She needs more successes, not failures, in order to gain confidence in herself.

Case example

Sharon readily agreed to take Antabuse to control her episodic drinking binges which put the children in jeopardy. The worker, alert to the fact that Sharon could not afford to fail one more time, reminded her what it means to be on Antabuse. It required daily attendance at a clinic located 8 miles away from the central city, a daily trip on a bus with 3 small children. The meeting she was to attend was held at 2.00-3.30 p.m. every day. This meant that Sharon would not be home when her 7-year-old returned home from school. Clearly, the worker and Sharon had to come up with some other, more realistic plan.

2. The goal must be positive replacement behaviour

The goal must be stated in concrete, measurable terms, as positive replacement behaviour, rather than an absence of negative, undesirable behaviour. A client saying things like "I will never do it again", "I will never get mad", "I will never let him in", "I will never leave the child alone" is not enough. It is unrealistic to think that she will remember not to do all these things in the heat of anger or frustration. The more concrete, detailed options the client has, the better. Therefore, you need to clarify the goal with the client by asking, "So, what would you do instead of getting mad (getting drunk, leaving the child alone, etc.)?" The process of having to describe these alternatives forces clients to think out aloud and thus realistic choices can be made.

Case example

Worker: So, when you discipline your child without violence, what would you do differently?

Linda : I will just have to not spank him.

Worker: I can see that it is important to you not to hit him. So, what do you suppose you will do instead of hitting when you get frustrated?

Client: Well, I will just walk out, count to ten, send him to his room and then talk to him later.

Discussion:

The client's vague idea of not hitting her child is translated into some concrete, behavioural replacement for hitting the child. It is always better not to accept vague, global ideas like "I will not spank him.", or "I will do better next time.", or "I won't drink any more." It is easier to recognise when a positive goal has been achieved than a negative one. That is, when the client does not hit the child, it is difficult for her to know that she is not hitting. If she sets herself goals such as "I will count to ten", "I will send him to his room", "I will walk out of the house", she will know when she is achieving her goal.

3. The goal must be important to the client

We all know that unless someone wants to change, it is impossible to force them to change. Since it is the client who has to make the needed changes, if at all possible, it is better for the worker to agree with what she wants to change, rather than tell her what to change.

The goals must be meaningful to the client and she must view the achievement of the goals as having some beneficial and positive results for her. For example, her involvement with the FBS may result in her child behaving better, doing better in school, increasing the chances of success in school and in life, or feeling good about herself as a mother, and so on.

What the client wants most might be for the worker to get out of her life and not come around to "bother" her. If this is the case, it is indeed a good goal. The worker's job is to be able to close the case and do it without jeopardising the safety of the children. Therefore, the worker and client want the same thing, that is, not to have to see each other for too long.

Case example 1

Worker: So what can I do that will be helpful to you?

Client: I want other people to stop messing with my life.

Worker: I think you are absolutely right. We want the same thing for you. We want to get out of your life as soon as possible. So, what do you have to do so that we don't have to meet like this?

Client: I suppose you have to think that I don't mess my kids up, which I don't.

Worker: I have to be able to report to my boss that you are managing your life in such a way that there is no danger of your child getting hurt. So, how badly do you want to get rid of me? (A scaling question would be very useful here. For instance, "On a scale of 1 to 10, where 10 means you will do damned near anything to get rid of me, and 1 means you will just sit around and wait for something to happen, where would you say you are today?")

Discussion:

Even though what the client wants does not come from the kind of motivation that we might wish, it is always much better to start "where the client is", and move on from there rather than trying to change her mind. When the worker "cooperates" with the client, it is much easier for her to "cooperate" with the worker. Once the client recognises that the worker has a genuine respect for what she feels is important and good for herself and her children, it is easier for her to move beyond insisting on her own agenda. Clients are very sensitive about subtle, non-verbal messages, therefore, be sure you believe in what you do and say.

Case example 2

Linda Turner, mother of 4 children aged from 14 to 4, was very angry and defensive when we first met her. All her children were removed when the oldest, Tish, reported abuse to the school. Because they could not find a foster home that could take all the children, they were placed in 3 different homes. She was court ordered to receive individual and family counselling with the children. After 6 months, Tish was the first to express desire to return home.

In order to gather information, we asked Linda about her contacts with various helping professionals. She described the family counselling she attends with 11-year-old Marcus as very upsetting because she somehow gets the impression that the counsellor only listens to Marcus and not to her concerns about his poor school work and the trouble he gets into at school since he has been at the foster home. She also complained a lot about various foster parents who treat her "like she is a criminal or something". She didn't like the social worker who "kept telling me what to do like I was ignorant or something".

Linda is a big, barrel-chested woman, and talked with a tough and booming voice, saying "I tells it like it is and don't beat around the bush". It was easy to believe her and at the same time, be easily put off by her. She almost invited similarly tough responses from those who worked with her. In addition, her "disciplinary" measures were very harsh and unrealistically demanding of children. Her view of the world was that one had to fight everything and everybody just to survive: "don't let anybody walk on you."

When asked the "miracle question" (see Chapter 6), she softened considerably and became teary-eyed, saying that she loves all her children and she wants all of them back with her but realised that she will have to do it with one child at a time.

Worker: What would it take you to do that?

Linda: I have to keep going to counselling, keep visiting my kids, go to parenting classes, learn to keep my temper under control, and keep my job.

Worker: So what is the first step you need to make?

Linda: I want Tish to come home first because she said now she wants to come home.

We decided that Linda's immediate goal was to have Tish come home first, and her plan to have one child returned at a time seemed reasonable and realistic.

4. The goal must be described as a beginning of new behaviour, not an end of something.

Clients often describe their goals in an idealistic, trouble-free, dream-like way. It can be a positive sign that the client sees the possibility of her life being different from what it is for her at the moment. However, as a goal, it could take a lifetime to achieve. Therefore, the client needs some assistance from the worker to start shaping a goal that is small, concrete, and important enough to her for her to put effort into.

Case example

Let us follow Linda as we try to negotiate the goal. Linda decided that having Tish come home first is what made sense to her. Now, Linda and the worker need to know what would be the first sign that will tell Linda that Tish is ready to come home, or for Linda to have Tish come home.

Worker: Linda, what would be the first thing that will let you know that Tish is ready to come home?

Linda: She's said it already. I never thought she would say it but she says she wants to come home.

Worker: So, let us look down the road a bit and think about this. Suppose she comes home first. What would be the first signs that tell you that you and Linda are going to make it so that she will not have to leave home again?

Linda: We will talk together more. She will tell me what's on her mind, what she needs from me, and not run off to my mother's. I will listen to her more. I will remember that she is a teenager and she has to wear teenage clothes. I will say this. I never talked to my mother because she didn't listen to me.

Worker: So, what else will tell you that you and Tish are going to make it this time?

Linda: I will know how to talk to her nice and not yell at her like she was my enemy or something.

Discussion:

As you listen to this exchange, it is clear that the worker is trying to help Linda recognise the early signs that she and Tish are starting a new pattern of interactions. As the conversation continues, the worker can elaborate on the details of the new relationship.

6. What if your goal and the client's goals are different?

If your view of what is the most urgent problem to solve differs from that of the client, clearly you need to establish priorities. Obviously, a child's safety has to come first and if the Child Protection assessment of risk judges it to be acute and the difference of goal remains unresolvable following attempts at recontracting, then the Child Protection Service must do whatever is necessary to ensure the safety of the child in question. But when a situation appears chronic and there is no immediate risk, it may be possible to work first on the client's goals. The experience of working together successfully on her goals is likely to make the client more willing to cooperate around your goals.

Even if your goals appear different to those of the client, frequently what the client wants and what you want are but differently framed expressions of the same goal. For example, the client reluctantly meets with you in order not to have the children taken away and your goal is to insure that the children are safe and reasonably well taken care of, by the biological parent if possible. Her goal may be to "stop the social service from coming around" and in order to achieve that, she must do certain things to meet the minimum standard of insuring safety and of child care.

C. INTERVIEWING AS AN INTERACTIONAL PROCESS

Professional interviewing is the process of interaction between a client who is seeking service and a professional person who has the knowledge and skills to provide it. Therefore, the worker uses interviewing as a major tool, not only to gather information but to direct the conversation towards the goal finding solutions.

The client-worker relationship remains a system for the duration of the contact, in which both worker and client influence, and are influenced by, each other. Therefore, when the worker behaves in a certain way, the client will react in a certain way, and vice versa. (See Chapter 1.) This is called the circular interactional process. Over time, this interactional pattern becomes a rule-governed, predictable, and repetitive system. The process of interviewing the client relies on this pattern of interaction.

Each participant in this interactional system has considerable influence on the on-going pattern of relationship, and at the same time, each is equally dependent on the other to make the system work. Since the purpose of the client-worker system is to benefit the client, it is the worker's job to figure out how to use the relationship to help the client achieve her goals. As you read through the next section, think of yourself as a finely tuned instrument of change for the client.

What To Do and What Not To Do

1. Many workers mistake the ventilation of feelings as the sole curative tool we have, and each session or contact becomes a "bitching session", or "letting it all hang out" becomes the goal. Just talking about feelings or looking into the client's past has limited usefulness since understanding feelings and gaining insight into their past will not change the future. Doing something about their lives changes their lives. It may be necessary to allow the client to vent a certain amount of frustration or anger in order to convey to the client that you are interested in her feelings and to acknowledge the difficult life she has had. However, she should not be allowed to wallow in how difficult her life has been, or what a lousy childhood she had, and so on, and use it as an excuse for why she cannot change her future and why she cannot be an adequate mother.

2. Whenever possible, direct the conversation to future action, using action oriented words, such as "So, what do you need to do so that you feel better about yourself?"

3. Be clear about your goal and keep it in mind at all times. Do not allow the client to drift around just filling the space with words. Each conversation you have with a client has a purpose and should lead in the general direction of finding ways to achieve the goal.

4. Phrase questions in such a way that the client elaborates on her thinking and her own ideas. Imagine yourself being a client in the following situations and notice the difference in the way you would respond when the question is phrased differently.

Worker: Do you know what you have to do so that you don't have to come here anymore?

When asked this way, the client has an option of saying "Yes" or "No", or "O-huh". When this happens, the burden of asking the follow-up question falls to the therapist, not the client. It is the client who should take the responsibility for change, not the therapist.

You can imagine what kind of questions the therapist will have to come up with to remind the client about what she has to do. Reminder: Whenever you find yourself asking the type of questions that the client can respond to with a simple "Yes" or "No" answer, you are already working too hard and the client not hard enough. When you find yourself doing this, change the direction as described in the following manner. Remember, it is the client who should work hard, not you.

"What do you suppose you have to do so that everybody can stay out of your life?", or "What do you suppose your parents will have to see you do so they get the idea that you don't have to come here anymore?"

"What do you think it will take for you to convince your neighbours that they do not have to call the welfare department? (or to leave you alone?)"

"What do you think will convince the teacher that you are taking care of your child and that she doesn't have to be concerned about your son?"

"What do you suppose will convince your mother (or sister, aunt, and so on) that you are starting to take care of your life?"

Do not be put off or discouraged with a passive response like,"I don't know" accompanied by a shrug of shoulders. Pretend that you are slow or dense and persist with a naive voice and rephrase the question. When the client figures you are not going to be put off that easily, she may decide that you passed the first test.

5. Whenever you ask a question, be clear in your mind how the answers to these questions will help direct the client towards thinking about finding solutions.
6. When clients go off at tangents, gently bring them back to the focus of the conversation.

   Example

   > "It's still not clear to me, Linda, what is it that you have to do so that people will leave you alone?"

   Or

   > "I want to come back to this, Linda, what will have to be different so that people will not bother you?"

7. It can be useful to deliberately appear "confused" about inconsistency or gaps in information. Clients are more likely to help a "confused" therapist than a "smart ass" one. It is not helpful to provoke or anger the clients.
8. When you need to confront, do not use accusative words or postures. Be sure your tone of voice is not angry or blaming. You are likely to create a "passive-

aggressive" client who knows how to defeat you. Just use simple, straightforward words like, "So, what do you have to do to stop your boyfriend abusing your child?"

9. Always keep in mind that it is better to have the client as an ally than as an adversary.

10. Always use neutral and positive words.

Example

Worker: I understand that some people have been very concerned about your family, concerned enough to ask us to look into your family. How can we help?"

11. Sometimes it is better to assume that they have asked for help and proceed with that assumption. It helps the client avoid having to ask for help all over again. The client may feel ashamed or humiliated about needing help, and nobody likes to have to ask for help.

Example:

Worker: I understand that you need some help to keep the family together. What do you think is the first thing you need help with?

Or

"It is not hard to see that you need some help with keeping your family together. What is the first thing you have to do so that your family can stay together?"

These approaches help the client and the worker to move right into the task of figuring out what the goals are and beyond. They allow some, not all, clients room to "save face". Some people are too proud to ask for help, or embarrassed about it being found out that they are not doing an adequate job with their children. We need to be sensitive to such common human emotions.

Six
USEFUL QUESTIONS AND OTHER INTERVIEWING TECHNIQUES

The worker's decision to ask certain questions and not others, may appear haphazard and random to the uninitiated. But each professional transaction between the worker and the client is a purposeful one, thus, which questions the worker decides to ask, how, when, and whom to ask or not, has significant impact on the client-worker relationship. At times, not asking certain questions has a more powerful impact on the client. Focusing on certain aspects of the client's life while ignoring others conveys certain messages and impressions to the client.

For example, when the worker asks the client a detailed question about her childhood experience of being physically abused by her mother, certain messages are conveyed to the client, such as, the worker views her history of abuse as an important link to her current abusive behaviour of her children. On the other hand, when the same worker asks the same client detailed information about how she managed to be so loving to her own child, it implies something else. The decision to ask certain questions and not others, must always be related to what the goals are.

As interviewing, the act of asking and answering questions, is the single most important tool the worker has, the topic merits our close attention. We need to look at what to ask when, how, and whom to ask, and for what purpose. This chapter describes and discusses ways to use 5 particularly useful questions. They are questions about past success, exception, miracle, scale, and coping.

A. QUESTIONS ABOUT PAST SUCCESSES AND PRE-SESSION CHANGE

PAST SUCCESS
Through the interviewing process, the worker can focus on the client's past successes, that is, when she was functioning well enough not to require community intervention. It is empowering for the client to discover that there was a period in her life when she was more successful than she feels at the moment. She needs help to remember these successful periods in her life, because it is easy for her to forget that she has functioned well in the past, especially while she is under the stress of dealing with social service systems and managing her life in the context of the very reason that brought her to the attention of the community. Once the forgotten and unused problem-solving skills are uncovered, the next task for the worker and the client is to find ways to adapt them to her current difficulties.

Furthermore, when the client "discovers" these small but significant successes she has had, it helps her to re-assess herself. This section will discuss and list examples of questions that elicit this helpful information and ways to make use of the client's past and current successes.

For example, imagine asking a client the following questions:

"The record indicates that 2 years ago you had your child returned to you from the foster home. What did you do right that time?"

and

"What do you suppose the social worker (or the court) thinks you did to convince them that you were ready to have your child returned?"

Or the following questions:

"The record indicates that the Department placed your child in a foster home. Do you remember why that happened?"

and

"What do you suppose the social worker thought was wrong with your parenting that made it necessary to take your child away from you?"

Discussion:

It is not difficult to see the difference between the first set of questions and the second set. The first set of questions acknowledges in a matter-of-fact fashion that her child was taken away from her and also the success of having her child returned. There is a less blaming tone to the interaction. When the worker decides to focus on her success in having completed the program to have the child "returned" to her, it effectively puts the past behind her and looks to the future.

The second set of questions emphasise that she had her children "taken away" from her and the guilt associated with the event. Questions related to "why" usually imply that there are knowable causes for the problem and place the blame on someone, usually the person being asked. It is clear that the question becomes rhetorical. The client knows that the worker knows the answer. These are small but significant differences that make a great difference when dealing with FBS clients.

When asked about her past successes or the times when she felt positive about herself, the client frequently becomes briefly disoriented and appears startled for few seconds. It is usually such an unexpected question from the worker. Many clients report that this is the first time they have been treated as having a brain or as having done some things right in their past. In fact, many clients become tearful, and then calmer, more cooperative, and often their expression and posture changes. It is easier for the client to become hopeful about herself when she can look back at her successful past and review the successes. The following are some examples of questions that the worker can ask.

Examples of Questions About Past Successes:.

"How did you manage to get out of that abusive relationship with Tyler? How did you find enough strength to get rid of him?"

"It is not easy to raise 3 children on your own. How did you do it?"

"After having been through what you've been through, how did you find enough strength to keep pushing on?"

"How come things aren't worse? How do you manage to keep going when there seems to be no hope?"

"What do you suppose you need to do so that you'll feel good about yourself and in control of your life again?"

"What would it take for you to get back the confidence you had when you were in high school?"

"What do you suppose your mother (sister, boyfriend, etc) would say you need to do to bring back your old self-confidence?"

Worker: How do you manage to force yourself to get up in the morning?

Client: It's only because I don't want my kids to drop out of school like I did.

Worker: You really want your children to do better than you have done. You must love them very much.

Client: They are all I have. I want them to get through school, get good jobs, have the good things that I can't have.

Worker: What are you doing so that you can continue to hope and to try one more time? What do you think your mother (or some other person important in the client's life) would say keeps you going?

Discussion:

These are some examples of how you can help clients regain self-confidence and help them realise that they still have the ability to shape their lives the way they want them to be.

All of the above questions can be phrased in such a way that a client can be detached enough to be observant of herself, and thus make rational, long-term decisions, and not react to the situation on an impulse based on emotions.

PRE-SESSION CHANGE

Since client and worker normally first meet because of a problem, it is all too easy to focus on the difficulty and to miss the fact that clients are likely to have already done things to diminish the problem. In fact, research (Weiner-Davis, de Shazer, and Gingerich, 1987) shows that clients describe exceptions and/or pre-treatment changes in at least two-thirds of cases. However, if you do not ask about pre-treatment change, clients will not tell you since they will not see them as relevant.

Case example : A New Life For Sharon

Sharon, aged 21, had 2 children, ages 4 and 14 months and was expecting her third child in about a month. Her relationship with Archie had been a turbulent one which had been frequently "on and off" for the past 3 years. Archie's problems with job instability, drinking, drug use, and fighting, led to frequent physical abuse of Sharon.

Sharon had a long history of rocky relationships with her divorced parents, with whom she had fought since her early 'teens. She said they had been always critical of her parenting, her choice of relationships with men, and numerous other issues.

Sharon reported that her mother had "nothing good" to say about her, and that her father said it was her fault that Archie mistreated her and pushed her around when he was drunk. Of course, Sharon had given them her share of grief; she started to run away at 13, played truant from school, flirted with drinking and drug use, became pregnant at 15, and eventually dropped out of school. She and her first child lived in a foster home because her parents refused to take her home from the hospital. She and Archie tried living together for a while but could not afford the housing. Sharon and Archie were currently living with their respective parents but acted as if they were "married".

Sharon same to the attention of FBS because her 4-year-old daughter was caught up in their most recent fight and sustained a minor injury. Between the run to the hospital, meeting with the Child Protection Service worker, getting ready for the imminent delivery, she decided that she and the children deserved something better than what they'd been getting from Archie, and announced that she was through with him.

So, what was different this time that made her think that she would follow through with her decision to break up with Archie? After all, she had done this on and off for 3 years, and she would soon have Archie's third child.

Sharon listed several different things she did the day before our first appointment; all new things she has never done before. She told Archie's mother off. She said it was pretty scary and took a lot of guts because Archie's mother was a "powerful lady" who screamed at her about her "selfishness" and the grandparent's right to see her grandchildren and threatened her with a court action to assert her rights.

She called the hospital where she planned to deliver her baby and arranged to have the baby placed in a special area that would allow only limited access to a special list of visitors. She calmly announced to Archie that their relationship was over and hung up on him when he started to cry and beg her to take him back. Sharon made an arrangement with friends to stay in phone contact in case she weakened and was tempted to take Archie back, or gave in to him when he begged. She said this was the first time she felt angry at him for refusing to take responsibility for her and the children. This was really the first time. She had always felt hurt in the past and had suffered quietly.

The worker decided to utilise her pre-session change and complimented and supported her decision to make a new life for herself and the children. The worker kept wondering what was different about yesterday that gave her the strength to make all these changes. She was not clear about what made the difference initially, but later began to form the opinion that the new baby on the way had made the difference. She felt that her 3 children needed more stability and responsible adults in their lives, and she realised that no matter how much she fought with Archie, he was not going to become responsible.

Since Sharon was so determined in her decision to remain strong, it was suggested that she kept track of what she did when she overcame the urge to either ask him to come back or take him back when he begged.

Sharon was beaming when the worker met her the following session. She went over all her meetings with Archie and reported that, although tempted many times to go back to the old ways, she had handled things differently, which had made Archie mad. Many things she did were new for her, such as going out with girlfriends, contacting old friends, making decisions independently of Archie, and telling him that he could not just come over on the spur of the moment.

She provided a good example of how she was handling things differently. Archie called and begged her to allow him to visit the children. Sharon said firmly that since he had not showed up for 3 weeks she was not going to allow him to "waltz in and out of their lives" and that he had to show her that he was committed to his children by demonstrating his ability to stick to regular visitation hours. He agreed to this and now comes only at the visitation hours to pick up the children, giving her a much needed break from them.

B. EXCEPTION FINDING QUESTIONS

"Exception" means times when the problem did not happen. The worker and the client need to examine who did what, how, when, and where so that the problem didn't happen, in other words, how the patterns around the problems were changed.

Case example

Every time 6-year-old Tyrone starts fighting, hitting his sister, and makes himself a nuisance, his grandmother grabs him, pulls him away, scolds him, and then he goes into a tantrum, crying, kicking, and turning blue. One day, the grandmother decided she was too tired to intervene and left them alone to fight it out. To her surprise, Tyrone started playing with his sister when Michelle ignored his usual invitation for fight.

In this example, there are several exceptions to their usual interaction sequences: grandmother's decision not to intervene in their fight; sister's spontaneous decision to ignore his invitation; and Tyrone doing something other than what he normally does. If all 3 people who are involved in this exception were to repeat this scenario, either together or separately, there is a good chance that they are likely to have a much more peaceful time when they are together.

WHEN PROBLEMS OCCUR IN LIMITED SITUATIONS

Frequently, problematic behaviours happen only within certain physical, relational, or topical contexts. In other words, Jamie loses his temper only at home and not at other places, such as at school, at church, or when at auntie's house. Jena becomes unmanageable only with with mother and not with mother's new boyfriend, or with a baby-sitter. Joe loses his temper and becomes violent only when he has been drinking quite a bit or when he discusses money with his wife. It is important to find out in detail what happens when the person does not have a problem since the client can learn to transfer the ability she uses successfully in one setting to another situation.

For example, the police were called to take Beverly to the County hospital. She "went on a rampage" and "trashed the house" when she got into another fight with her husband. She readily agreed that she "just lost it" and really could not afford to keep doing it. Beverly acknowledged that she had always had a hot temper since she was a child. In the process of looking for exceptions to her 'hot temper" it was learned that she held her job at a warehouse of a large grocery store chain for three years and that she "loved working there". She was considered a good employee, and had never lost her temper with her supervisor or co-workers, even though they were "rowdy, condescending, macho guys" who teased her for being a woman. Looking at this as an exception, the worker and Beverly found many ways she managed to control her temper and "keep her cool" even when she could have easily lost her temper with her co-workers.

17-year-old Michael was described as a hostile, aggressive young man who had poor impulse control. He cut classes, flunked most classes year after year; was unmanageable at home and in the community with a long list of problematic and delinquent behaviours, such as running away, truancy, stealing, breaking and entering, using and dealing in drugs. Many attempts to solve his problems through various treatments failed. After holding up an old lady, he finally ended up a correctional institution. where he earned praise for good behaviour and academic achievements. He made a model student, worked in the cafeteria, participated in sports activities, and earned privileges for a week-end furlough after 4 months, which was thought to be amazing, given his destructive past behaviours.

Giving recognition for successful periods in their lives, and acknowledging a client's ability to function in a competent fashion, even in limited areas, is helping the client get started in the right direction. Clearly, the next task for the worker is to encourage the client to maintain and increase the number of areas in which she is successful.

WAYS TO ASK QUESTIONS

The following are examples of questions designed to help a client discover her own strengths and abilities to solve problems on her own. Even when the success may be very small compared to the numerous problems the client faces, solution starts with small steps.

It is always better for the client to come up with her own solutions rather than being told what to do. When it is her own idea, she is more likely to be committed to successful solutions. In addition, if a solution is generated from within the client's existing resources, it fits naturally with her way of doing things, and it is easier to do more of. Furthermore, when the solution is more congruent with her life-style than any newly learned behaviour, she is less likely to relapse.

Examples of Questions

Worker: I can see that you have every reason to be depressed. So when do you suppose you get a little bit less depressed?

Client: Well, I'm not sure. I get depressed all the time. I feel a little bit better when I have some money to spend on my kids. I feel like I am a better mother when I can buy things for my kids.

Worker: So, what would you say is different with you when you can buy things for your children?

Client: Well, then I feel like I'm a good mother. I hate being poor because it reminds me of my own mistakes. I feel worse at the end of the month when I run out of money.

Worker: So how would you say you are different when you are a little bit less depressed?

Client: Well, I force myself to get up in the morning even when I don't feel like it, get the kids ready for school, maybe even get a little bit more cheerful when I force myself, maybe even walk to school with the kids, and get out of the house. Then I can forget how depressing my life is.

Worker: So, when you don't force yourself, what do you suppose your children notice different about you?

Client: I try not to show them. But I suppose they know. Sometimes when I don't get out of bed in the morning, the children fight more.

Worker: So, what would it take for you to force yourself to get up in the morning more often?

Discussion:

As you can see from the exchange, the worker ignored some issues that the client has no control over at the moment, such as, not having money, having made mistakes, and instead concentrates on her current small but useful successes. When the client forces herself to get up in the morning, things generally turn out little better. Clearly, the client needs to repeat this.

More Examples:

Worker: You are saying that you didn't drink for 5 days last week. How did you do it? I am amazed that you controlled your drinking for 5 days. How did you do it?

Client: It's only 5 days. I've gone longer than that when I was pregnant.

Worker: You did? How did you do that? Wasn't it hard? You mean you did it all alone without going into treatment? How long did you not drink for that time?

Client: Well, I didn't want to hurt my baby when I was pregnant. It was hard at first but I just told myself I'm not going to do it. So, when I'd go out, I used to drink soda.

Worker: That's amazing. You must be a strong person. Now, tell me how you didn't drink for 5 days this time.

Client: I didn't have any money. I was broke.

Worker: Come on, I know that if you really wanted to drink, you would have found ways to get that drink. How did you manage not to drink?

Later in the session the following questions can be asked:

"Tell me, what is different for you at those times when you do not drink?"

"How do you explain to yourself that the problem doesn't happen at those times?

"Where did you get the idea to do it that way?"

"What do you suppose your mother (boyfriend, husband, etc.) would say you do differently when you do not drink?

"What will have to happen for you to do it more often?"

"What else would you say you do differently when the problem doesn't happen?"

"What will you and your boyfriend do differently when the problem doesn't happen?"

Answers to these questions are followed with questions like:

"So, what do you have to do so that you can continue to say "No" to drinking? (or whatever the client says she does to have successes)

"What do you suppose you and your children (or boyfriend) will be doing differently instead of drinking (getting depressed, etc)?

"If your boyfriend were here and if I were to ask him, what do you suppose he would say he notices different about you when you do not drink (get depressed, act angry, etc)?

"What would he say has to happen for that to happen more often?"

"How long would they say this has to continue for them to get an idea that your problem is solved?"

"When the problem is solved, how do you think your relationship with your (mother, sister, friend, etc.) will change? What will you be doing then that you are not doing now?"

Discussion:

As you can see, the worker here is trying very hard to give the client credit for her own success while getting her to realise that it was something she did rather than waiting for something to happen to her.

In the process of having to explain to the worker, it becomes more and more clear to the client that she did something to create an exception to the problem. She can own up to her success. It is easier to own up to her failures when she can own up to the success first. It also means that she can repeat the successful behaviour.

The next task for the worker is to find ways to reinforce her success and amplify it by increasing her self-confidence and self-esteem.

C. MIRACLE QUESTIONS

Getting the client to imagine that a miracle has happened and her problem is solved has a powerful clinical impact on the client. First, it creates a vivid image or vision of what her life will be like when the problem is solved, and second, she can see some hope that life can be different from what it is.

The question goes like this: "Suppose one night there is a miracle while you are sleeping (or suppose a fairy godmother waves her magic wand) and the problem that brought you to the attention of FBS is solved. Since you are sleeping, you don't know that a miracle has happened and that your problem is solved. What do you suppose you will notice different the next morning that will tell you that there has been a miracle?"

Client reactions vary. Some clients start to look up, break out into a broad smile, their eyes brighten up, they sit up straight, and start to describe in detail how their lives will be transformed. Some clients are genuinely surprised at their own words of hope, some listen attentively to their family members' descriptions of miracles for themselves as well as for others. Some clients are unable to imagine how their lives would change, even with coaxing and help.

Some clients initially talk about winning a lottery, or other "pie in the sky" pipe dreams and then they usually settle down to become much more realistic. They begin to describe how their lives will change in concrete, specific, small, and achievable terms. Help the client describe the imagined changes in as much detail as possible. Clearly, the first therapeutic task is to elicit this information in such a way that the client can see the possibility of her "miracle" really happening. The next task is to help the client figure out what might be the initial steps she can take to initiate those behaviours that will lead to "miracles".

Examples of Questions and Answers:

Client: I will have a job, have a nice place to live, nice clothes, will have a man who cares about me, not just uses me but really cares about me. My children will be happy, they will do well in school. Maybe I will be in school so that I will get a training to get a job.

Worker: Well, that sounds like at the end of a big miracle. What do you suppose is the first thing - in the morning - that will tell you "Hey, something is different in my life"?

Client: Well, I will get up earlier, have some time for myself, say good morning to the kids with a smile, get them up, sit down with them for breakfast, tell them to have a good day and send them off to school.

Worker: If you were to pretend that the miracle has happened, what would be the first thing you would do?" (This is a strong suggestion that the client has to do something to solve the problem).

What would it take to pretend that this miracle has happened? Anything else? What else?

If you were to do that, what would be the first change you would notice about yourself?

Who would be the first person to notice next day that something is different about you after the miracle?

What would your mother (husband, friend, sister, etc.) notice different about you, if you didn't tell her that there'd been a miracle? What else? Anything else?

What would your mother (or others) do differently then?

What do you think will be different between you and your mother then?

If you were to take these steps, what would you notice different around your house?

If you were to do that, what would be the first thing your children would notice different around your house? (Again a strong suggestion that the client can do something).

What would they do differently then? (Again a strong suggestion that she should look for different, more positive behaviour in the children.) What else? Anything else?"

What else would be different in your household?

Discussion:

You may have noticed that these examples use the words "different" and "change" quite frequently. They are very purposely designed to suggest that a), the client has to do things "differently" in order to bring about changes in her life, b), that she is the one who has to do them, she has to take an active role in reshaping her life, and c), that it is her responsibility to do so. At the same time, the questions are aimed at trying to elicit her own ideas of the form of the solution. Answering these miracle questions will provide her with clues on what first step she needs to take to find solutions and show her how her life will change, thus motivating her and giving her hope that her life can change.

MIRACLE QUESTIONS FOR GOAL SETTING PURPOSES

Depending on how the worker phrases the questions, the answers to miracle questions can be a useful guide to the general direction in which the client wants to change her life. (See Chapter 5 on goal setting.)

D. SCALING QUESTIONS

Scaling questions have been found to be very versatile. Because they are simple, we find that children old enough to understand number concepts (that 10 is greater than 5, for example), respond very well. Adults whose thinking style tends to be concrete, precise, and pragmatic, and who are generally thought to be poor candidates for psychotherapy, also respond very well. It is simple to keep track of and does not require sophisticated intellectual power to comprehend. Since culturally (at least in western society) we tend to view 10 as bigger, better, and higher than 1, I have used the scale in a straightforward manner. Therefore, the most desirable state is placed at 10, while 1 indicates the opposite.

As you will notice, scaling questions can be used to assess the client's self-esteem, self-confidence, investment in change, willingness to work hard to bring about desired changes, prioritizing of problems to be solved, perception of hopefulness, evaluation of progress, and so on - things considered too abstract to concretise. It also helps the client to assess what significant others in her life think about these situations.

This question has wide application. The more you experiment with it, the more proficient you will become at using it. You will find that only your creativity will limit its usefulness. Experiment and play with it. One word of caution: you may have to specify time limits, such as "today", "last week", "during the past month". Without that limit, clients become confused. When the worker specifies the focus in such time-limited fashion, the client finds the questions much more useful since she is not committing herself to an indefinite future or the past.

OUTLOOK ON PROBLEM SOLVING

Worker: On a scale of 10 to 1, with 10 meaning you have every confidence that this problem can be solved, and 1 meaning no confidence at all, where would you put yourself today?"

Client: I would say 5, in the middle.

Worker: On the same scale, how hopeful are you that this problem can be solved?

Client: I would say 6.

Worker: What will be different in your life when you move from 6 to 7?

Worker: If your boyfriend (or mother) were here and I were to ask him (or her), where would he (or she) put the chances of this problem being solved?

Client: I'm not sure but I would guess that he would say it is at 3.

Worker: What will it take him to say it's at 4?

Client: He thinks I have to stop drinking.

Worker: So, how interested are you in wanting to stop drinking?

Client: I have to stop drinking. It's killing me, I know.

Worker: So, what is the first thing you have to do, Susan, to stop drinking?

Client: I just have to stop drinking when I get upset.

Worker: What do you suppose your boyfriend would say is the first step for you, Susan, to stop drinking?

Discussion:

As you can see from this exchange the worker here is using the numbers to gather information about how much support the client is getting from her environment, and this eventually helps the client to talk about the steps she needs to take towards solving the problem.

The more the client is encouraged to say what she has to do, will do, needs to do, the more she believes it is her idea to stop drinking. Repetition of the same question in several different ways is a good way to reinforce and support client decisions.

MOTIVATION

"On the same scale, how much would you say you are willing to work to solve this problem?"

"Where do you suppose your mother (or some significant other) would say you are at?"

"Where would you put your husband on the same scale?"

The closer to 10 the client is, the more invested she is. When a client gives a low number on the same scale, it can be followed up with:

"What do you suppose they would say you need to do to move up 1 point on the same scale?"

"What do you suppose they would say they need to see you do for them to get the idea that you are at 6?"

"What would it take for you to move up from 5 to 6?" or "When you move from 5 to 6, what will you be doing that you are not doing now?" (...from 6 to 7?)

"When you move from 5 to 6 (or 6 to 7), what will others notice different about you that they don't notice now? What do you suppose you will notice different about them,then?"

"How invested would your husband would say he is, on the same scale, in helping you solve this problem?"

"How do you explain that he is more interested in you changing than you are? What do you suppose he would say is the reason that he is so interested in you moving from 5 to 6?"

Discussion:

Asking these questions is important in helping the client become more aware of her current position, where she wants to get to, what she is doing that helps, what she will need to do, and how the people around her might notice difference and respond differently as she changes, thus enabling her to make an informed decision on what step she needs to take.

SELF-ESTEEM

Worker: Let's say, 100 means you have become the ideal kind of person you always wanted to be, how close would you say you are to being 100 today?"

Client: I would say 35. I am not feeling too hot today.

Worker: On the same scale, what would you say was the closest to being 100 you ever came?

Client: I would say 70. That was two years ago.

Worker: What was going on in your life then?

Client: I was more confident about myself then. I was going to school, felt good about myself, I had hope and I knew I could do it.

Worker: What would it take for you to move closer to 70.

Client: I know what I have to do. I just have to do it. God, it's like it was 100 years ago but it was only two years ago. I was a good student, I had ambition. I could see where I was going.

Worker: So, what do you have to do to move up from 35 to 40?

Client: That's easy. I just have to get up every day at the same time and force myself to go look for a job.

Worker: So, when you get up at the same time and force yourself to look for a job, what do you suppose you will notice different about yourself?

Discussion:

As the above dialogue indicates, the worker does not have to know details of the client's past or the content of her problem in order to help her figure out what she has to do. The client has a clear sense of what she needs to do to get herself moving on the right path.

The last question the worker asked forces the client to imagine how she will be different when she actually does what she knows she has to do. This is a powerful motivator, particularly when she can see what lies beyond the hard work of making the necessary changes.

The following are more examples on the same theme that can be used to help the client to be motivated:

Worker: Let's say 10 means you feel the best you can imagine feeling about yourself, and 1 means the worst, what is the highest you ever felt about yourself?

Client: I would say 7.

Worker: What were you doing differently at the time?

or

What was going on in your life at the time?

or

What do you suppose your mother would say she noticed different about you in those days?

Discussion:

Whatever the client's answers are, the worker can usually find ways to encourage her to take steps toward repeating the 7 again. Even if the client is not ready to take steps to move back to 7 at this time, at least she has a chance to review the successful period in her life and remember all the good things she did to arrive at 7. This is something she did at one time, thus, the potential for her to repeat this is already there. This is an example of utilising past successes.

"What would it take for you to repeat that?"

"When the figure improves 1 point, (for example, from 3 to 4), what will be going on in your life that is not going on now?"

"What is the first step you need to take to make it happen now?"

"When you move up that 1 point, what will your mother (or some others) notice about you that's different?"

"What will she do differently when she notices that?"

"What was the lowest you ever felt about yourself? What did you do to get out of that?"

ASSESSMENT OF PROGRESS

Scaling questions can also be used to assess the client's perception of the progress she is making with the FBS program. The following examples show a number of different ways this question can be applied.

"Let's say, 10 is where you want your life to be and 1 is where we started our work together, where would you say you are at today?"

"Where do you suppose your mother would say you are at?"

"What has to be different in your life for you to say that you are 1 point higher?"

"What will it take you to move it up 1 point?"

"What do you suppose your mother would say you need to do to move up 1 point?"

"When you move up 1 point, who will be the first to notice the change?"

"When you move up 1 point, what will he/she notice different about you that he/she doesn't see now?"

"When your mother notices these differences in you, what do you suppose she will do differently with you?"

"When that happens, what will you do to let her know that you like what she is doing?"

"What do you suppose she will do then?"

"At what point do you think you will say we don't have to meet like this?"

"When things are at 7 or 8, what will be different with you that will tell you that you can go on with your life without outside help?"

Case example

The following is an example of the treatment of a family whose presenting problem centred on the problems of 12-year-old Timmy.

Worker: What do think you will notice different when Timmy moves up from 6 to 7?

Client: I will be able to trust him enough to go to a shopping mall without getting worried about him stealing things.

Worker: When you can do that, what else will you notice different about him that will tell you that it's OK to take him to a shopping mall?

Client: Well, he will come home on time, not fight with his brother, clean his room, take care of the dog mess in the yard, and not get phone calls from the teacher every day.

Worker: That sounds more like 8 or 9 than 7 to me.

Client: I guess you are right. I promised to take him fishing when he gets to be 8 or 9."

Discussion:

These are some examples of questions the worker can ask to assess what the client's perceptions are about her own or someone else's progress in treatment. The case example described above is an example of how to help a client have a more realistic expectation of the child's behaviour without getting into lecturing the parents.

ASSESSMENT OF RELATIONSHIP

"On the same scale, how much would he say he wants this marriage (or relationship)? How much would he say you want this marriage?"

"How much would you say you want this marriage to work out? How much do you think he wants to work on this marriage?"

"How do you explain that you want this marriage more that he does?"

"What do you know about this marriage that he doesn't, that makes you more invested in it?"

The same can be asked about the absent partner's perception by asking questions in the following manner:

"What would he say he knows about this marriage that you don't know that makes him so realistic?" (or optimistic or pessimistic, depending on situation)

"From his point of view, what do you suppose he would say it would take for him to want this marriage as much as you do? What else?"

Discussion:

As you can see, the value of scaling questions is limitless. It allows you to find out about all kinds of vague concepts or ideas that clients cannot explain. These questions help make things more concrete, and thus change and progress are easier to notice and to measure.

APPLICATION WITH CHILDREN

My clinical experience is that children as young as 7 or 8 years old can easily use scaling questions. It is more helpful, however, to use a visual scale, using a blackboard or writing pad, and draw a line from left to right or from the bottom to the top.

starting point X ——————————————— X goal

You might want to explore their perceptions by using the width of your arms as a measure, or using the floor as 1, moving up in the air, using a rising motion.

Case example

Eight-year-old Melissa, a bright and delightful child, was brought to therapy because she was molested in a shopping mall. After several sessions, she was making good progress. During the 5th session the therapist decided to ask her, using scaling questions, how much progress she thought she was making in therapy.

It was explained to Melissa that 10 meant her life would go back to normal, as it was before the incident, and 1 meant where she was when she first started to come to see the therapist. Drawing a line across from left to right on a writing board, the therapist asked where she thought she was on the line. She indicated her progress to be about 7.

1 ————————————————X———————10

Therapist: What do you suppose it will take you to go from here to there? (indicating point 10)

Melissa thought and thought for a long time and then finally said:

Melissa: I know what.

Therapist: What?

Melissa: I will burn the clothes I was wearing when it happened.

Therapist: What a wonderful idea! Melissa, I think that's exactly the right thing to do.

The therapist suggested to the mother that they devise a ritual around burning of the clothes as a family, followed by a celebration, such as going out to a fancy restaurant.*

E. COPING QUESTIONS

Every once in a while, FBS workers run into situations where a client has experienced extreme deprivation or a personal history that is fraught with high risk for abuse or mental illness. As a result workers can feel utterly hopeless about the client's future. When faced with such a situation, the most common reaction is to reassure the depressed and hopeless person, trying to cheer them up by saying things like, "Everything will turn out all right", or "Don't worry, look at the positive side", "You have so much going for you, look at yourself", and so on. The frustrating thing is that the client is not reassured; if anything, she becomes more hopeless, and often says even more desperate things.

Coping questions, when used properly, can be an empowering and uplifting experience for the client. The goal for the worker, as with all the other questions described in this book, is to help the client discover her own resources and the strengths she did not know that she had.

Client: It's no use. I have messed up my life and nothing is going to get better. Maybe I am just 'no good and will never amount to anything' like my mother always told me."

At this point, the worker has several options:

a) try to reassure her one more time and see what happens,

b) change the subject and distract her to some other topic,

c) reframe the strong faith she has in her mother's assessment of her as an expression of her loyalty toward her mother, for example, we will discuss "reframing" in Chapter 9), or

d) use coping questions as in the following example.

Case example 1

Worker: Since you are the kind of person who believes what your mother said about you, I can see how discouraged you can become about yourself. So, tell me, Helen, how do you keep going, day after day, when there is no hope for you. How do you even manage to get up in the morning?

Client: I don't get up every day like I should.

Worker: How did you manage to get yourself up this morning?

Client: I forced myself to get up because the baby was hungry and she was crying.

Worker: I can imagine how tempted you must have been to just to give up. What did you do to get up and feed your baby?

Client: Well, I had to. I love my baby. I don't want her to be hungry.

Worker: Is that what keeps you going, that you love your baby?

Client: That's the only thing that keeps me going. I don't want her to live with my mother if I'm not here.

Worker: You must love your baby very much. You are a very loving mother, aren't you?

Client: Well, that's the only thing that keeps me going.

Discussion:

As you can see from this exchange, the worker accepted the client's view that she believed her mother saying that she was "no good and will never amount to anything", and went beyond it by forcing Helen to come up with her own reason for getting up every day - her love for her baby. Until then, Helen had not thought about this aspect of herself - that she had enough strength to love her baby so deeply that she forced herself to get up every day.

The next task for the worker is to expand on this and to build on it.

Worker: So, what would it take you to keep doing what you've been doing?

Client: I will just have to force myself to do it. I will just have to remember that my baby needs me.

Worker: So, what would it take you to convince yourself that you are a good mother to your baby?

Client: I do all I can right now. I don't listen to my mother no more. I used to believe her, but I decided that she doesn't really know me. I don't want my baby to turn out to be like me.

Discussion:

You can see that Helen is beginning to map out what is good for her baby and make some decisions for her baby's sake. Meanwhile, the worker is working to help Helen to assert herself through feeling comfortable about having ideas about herself that are different from her mother's. There are many small things she is doing that are good for her, such as her decision not to listen to her mother any more. The worker can start to build on her strength, that is, her desire to do well with her baby, using it as a motivating force. Once she begins to feel good about herself as a mother, she will begin to make decisions based on her self-image as a "good mother".

Another example of using coping questions to turn a hopeless and overwhelming situation into something workable follows:

Case example 2

Client: I was beat up by my father when I was growing up. When he got drunk, he would wake me up in the middle of the night, holler at me, beat me up for no reason. He called me names. My mother would be so scared that she didn't say anything, She'd tell me to just do what my father wanted me to do, that I should let him molest me when he got drunk. Now, I don't trust men; I don't know how to love them, I don't know how to find a good man. I am like my mother; I let men use me and they take advantage of me. George will beat the crap out of me if I don't give him money so he can get his drugs. But I make sure that he don't get near my daughter."

Worker: How did you learn to cope with such a terrible situation all by yourself, with no help?

Client: I had to. I had no choice, did I?

Worker: I'm amazed that you not only cope with such a terrible situation with George but that you have enough strength to protect your daughter so that she doesn't get abused like you did. How do you do it?

Discussion:

This could help the client to see that she has considerable strengths and resources to build on. Returning to the Case Example 1, expanding on a client's strength can go like this:

Worker: So, how did you figure out, Helen, that you wanted to be a different kind of mother to your baby than your mother was to you? Where did you learn to do that?

Client: Well, I watch other people, read magazines, watch TV programs, and I think about it all the time.

Worker: You are a very thoughtful person. Have you always been that way, or is it something you learned to do?

Client: I had to learn myself. Nobody taught me how to do it.

Worker: That's fantastic. I'm sure someday, your baby will learn that from you.

Discussion:

As you can see from this exchange, even thou h the client feels hopeless about herself, the worker began "where the client was" and went on to help the client discover her fierce love for her child and her drive to become a different kind of mother from the mother she had. This is a powerful discovery for the client. More on when and how to use "coping questions" will be shown when we discuss crisis management.

F. WHEN NOT IF

You may have noticed in examples many instances of the worker asking questions that start with "When things are better...", "When you move up from 5 to 6 . . .." or "When you pretend the miracle has happened". "Who will be the first to notice when you feel better about yourself?" This is done deliberately, not by accident.

The use of when and not if is has the subtle but powerful implication that the changes described in the same sentence are bound to happen in time. The feeling conveyed to the client is that "of course it will happen" or "Of course you will make these changes, it's only a matter of time." Therefore, I suggest that you highlight when whenever possible to convey to the client that she will make some necessary changes.

In contrast, if is useful when the worker wants to express doubts about a hypothetical situation, that is, of a client having a setback, a slip back, or a minor relapse. This will be particularly useful when the client's history indicates that she has made many successful attempts but has been unable to maintain them. When the client is aware of her own weakness or vulnerability, she may be able to prepare herself, to prevent herself falling into the same trap again. If is also used to caution a client about normal setbacks and the ups and downs of everyday life. When she is reminded of the normal good days and bad days of everyday life, she is less likely to panic or overreact to them when they occur.

Frequently, a client who has recently started to abstain from drug or alcohol use has unrealistically high confidence that she can maintain her "clean" life by simply maintaining a high level of "strong will". In such a situation, you might want to say things like, "If you are to have a set back, do you have any idea what will be the first small sign to you?" or "If you have a set back and your depression starts to come back, what do you need to do to catch yourself so that you don't go all the way down?"

When you think the client is not clear about what the early signs of a minor setback might be, that is, when she starts to repeat the earlier patterns that got her in trouble, it will be valuable to discuss two things: a) what are the early signs, and b) how she will manage it if it comes.

For more ideas on how to manage the setback when it actually occurs, see Chapter 10 on Drug and Alcohol Abuse.

G. HOW TO END AN INTERVIEW

Closure of a session is just as important as the beginning. It is important to end the session not only with an upbeat note and a feeling of having accomplished something, but with some concrete plans for what is going to happen between sessions: that is, what step is required next to move towards the goal.

As you plan to wind down the session, the following ideas will help increase your effectiveness:

a) The length of the session - how long is appropriate.

b) Review of the goal for the session - have you achieved what you and the client set out to do?

c) Review what is the next step: Where do we go from here? What is client's task? What is your next task?

d) How close are we to termination?

1. The Length of An Interview

Unlike the common belief that the more "needy" the client, the longer time you must "give" to her, I contend that more is not necessarily better. Sometimes, a 30 minute session of focused effort is much more impactful for the client than 1 1/2 to 2 hours of meandering around various issues with no focus. Especially for those clients who have difficulty concentrating, it is much better to have a brief review of what the task was, what the result was, what the next step will be and end the session. This is more productive, professional, and an economical use of the worker's time.

2. Summarise The Session

At the end of the interview, it may be useful to review what was discussed during the session, remind them of the task, and what the next step is. Then decide on the next task and set up the next appointment.

During the summary, be sure to cover the following:

a) Remind the client of her successes, tasks accomplished, how hard she worked, how much she cares about her children, all the good things she has accomplished and a list of strengths. Again, all clients need reminders about these because it is difficult for them to see their own achievements.

b) The client needs to be praised for any tasks she did, on her own or as a result of following your suggestion. Always attribute a positive motivation for her willingness in doing the task. If she followed your suggestion with some modifications, praise her common sense, intelligence, and her intuition, to have done things in her own way. Give her the credit even if the credit is yours.

For those situations where the client did not do the task, see Chapter 8 for what to do.

c) Remind her what you are both aiming for next. The scaling question may be useful here to have her evaluate her own successes.

Case example

Worker: Suppose when we started, your problem with Tommy was at 1 and where you wanted to be at was at 10, how far do you feel you have come between 10 and 1 today?"

Client: I would say it's at 6. He still don't listen to me.

Worker: Of course, he is a teenager. What will he be doing different when you can say you are at 7?

Discussion:

You can give some informal education about unrealistic expectations clients have about themselves or of their children by agreeing with them and then "normalising" what she is complaining about. (See Chapter 9 on "normalising".)

3. Compliment at the end of a session

The compliment could be something as simple as "Shirley, you have come a long way and you are doing many good things for your children, like making sure that they get to school on time. It takes a lot of commitment and caring on your part and I'm just really impressed by you. Keep doing it. You are doing well. I know someday your children will realise how much you've done for them."

Sometimes, this is enough to make some clients become tearful, get choked up and appreciate you. This is probably rare appreciation, the kind of "pat on the back" they don't get from anyone, especially not the "social worker from the welfare department".

4. Reminder about termination

As each session becomes an occasion for evaluation and review of progress, both the worker and clients are reminded about how close they are coming to termination. Any termination should not come abruptly at the end of a set period and it should not come as a surprise either. It does not mean that the client will never have problems again, it just means that the client solved small but significant problems and in the process she learned a great deal about how to find solutions.

Seven
CONDUCTING A FAMILY SESSION

A. TECHNIQUES OF CONDUCTING FAMILY SESSIONS

The "family" in this chapter is used to mean the cross-generational unit, (whether chosen on legal, biological, or sociological grounds), the same-generation unit, or whoever the client designates as her "family". In some cultures, the "family" may mean the affectional unit, composed of close friendships. We will use the client's definition of the "family", and it therefore can be the parent-child unit, the grandparent-parent-child unit, other relatives of the client, her husband's relatives, husband-wife unit, "sister" and "brother" of non-biological unit, or live-in relationships of various durations.

Gathering together the clan of a large number of family members or other interested persons in the client's life is not an easy task to accomplish. It requires coordination of everyone's schedules, arrangement for transportation, child care, and the goodwill of everyone. The family session can take place when:

a) The client decides to bring her family members, either because a family member is problematic or because she believes that family members will be helpful in solving problems.

b) You request the client gathers together certain designated family members to come to the session, implying to the client that either a family member is a help or a hindrance to achieving the client's goals.

Some FBS, in-patient, outpatient, or residential treatment programs make the family involvement a necessary condition for participation in the treatment program.

Whatever the situation, the family session can be very productive when conducted well. It depends a great deal on your skill in capitalising on whatever goodwill there is among the family members and towards you. This section will describe ways to conduct the session in such a manner that it produces a positive outcome.

LENGTH OF TIME

To maximise the benefit of the session, allow yourself and the family about 1 to 1½ - hours for a family session. Less than this seems not enough; a longer period makes it difficult to hold everyone's attention. In an acute crisis situation, you may need longer than that to arrive at some resolution of the crisis.

HOW TO BEGIN

If you called the meeting, there should be some introductory comment from you about why you called the meeting and what you hope to accomplish by it. You can also ask them if they have any concerns about the family member with "the problem". Since you want to "join" with each member present, you need to thank them for coming, and offer some comment about how much they must care about the client as they were willing to extend their help. It is also a good idea to elicit each participant's idea about what he or she hopes to accomplish through such meetings.

NEUTRAL POSITION OF THE THERAPIST

An important thing to keep in mind during the family session is to maintain a neutral position by seeing the value of each participant's point of view. Once you take sides with someone, often the side of the the child against his/her parent or the side of a school against a parent, you are likely to lose your effectiveness. This can happen without your being aware of your own behaviour. You might get a nagging feeling that something is not quite right. Do not ignore these important intuitive cues.

So, how can you tell you are taking sides? The first clue is that you begin to think like one of the family members: you start to blame someone in the family, think in "right and wrong" terms, or become emotionally upset with some member of the family. Another important clue is that you start to find fault with one member of the family, start to say to yourself or to others how "disturbed" a person is, how serious the problem is, or spend much time analysing one member of the family.

What to do when you become aware of this happening to you? First, consult with the team, supervisor, or a consultant between sessions; second, review your notes and look for something good that person is doing, however small. Thinking about how you would reframe what that person (who you don't like) is doing as positive is also a good technique. If you feel strongly identified with one side of the family against the other, you need to think about how a larger picture of the system might fit together. Keep trying until you feel comfortable with it.

MAKE CONTACT WITH EACH PERSON

Make sure you take time to establish personal contact with each person by asking what their interest is, what they do that is fun, what they are good at, and so on, to convey to them that you are interested in them as a person. Again, remember to use everyday conversational language in a casual, relaxed manner. This conveys your authority and expertise in a personable, friendly way.

WAYS TO CONTROL THE FLOW OF CONVERSATION

Sometimes, conducting a family session is like being a traffic cop. Interaction among family members seems to have a life of its own. And indeed, it does. With or without you there, family life goes on; it has done and it will continue after you leave. Your goal is to minimise the family conflict, increase the positive feelings for each other, improve their ability to solve problems on their own, and improve their functioning, by having a conversation amongst themselves with you as the guide.

The decision to include small children in family sessions depends on what your focus and goals for the session are, and how helpful or distracting the presence of children is for what you are trying to accomplish. If the child is the focus of the work, you certainly may want to include children if they are old enough to express themselves. Sometimes it works better when small children are excused from the session.

The level of noise, or very disruptive interaction between family members certainly must be minimised in order for the session to be useful. There are no hard and fast rules about it: you must use your own common sense judgment about what needs to be done. It is always better for the parents to control their own children, perhaps with the worker's help rather than the worker directly trying to control the child. The task of FBS is to empower parents so that they can be in charge of their lives, including their children.

THE FOCUS OF THE FAMILY SESSION

The family session needs to focus on who needs to do what, how, when, and in what sequence in order to achieve what goal. To do this this, you need to a have clear sense about where the strength is, who is most willing to help, what the family's view of the "miracle" picture is, and what the first step is for those present.

In the family session, it is important for the worker to respect the family hierarchy. Since in family relationships the parents have more power, and if they don't they certainly should have more power than the child, more influence and hopefully the capacity and willingness to help their children do better, it is important to make sure that they experience the worker as wanting to support them in parenting more successfully, and as understanding the difficulties of their position.

So, address the parents first or take the position of consulting them about what is good for their child; give credit to them for having done some good things with their children. When referring to the parent in front of the children, it is more respectful to call them "Mother", "Father", "Mum" or "Dad", or to call them by their surnames, instead of calling them by their first names.

WAYS TO CONTROL INTENSE EMOTIONS

All families have had a long and varied history before you came on the scene, and it will continue long after their contact with you ends. All families have both positive and negative feelings towards each other, and whereas sharing sadness, tragedy or triumph can stimulate care, concern, and acceptance of one another, some issues can create a volatile, intensely emotional reaction of frustration, anger or disappointment.

Outbursts of emotional reaction in the session are rarely helpful,. unless you have some definite strategy and the skills to control and use the outburst therapeutically for everyone's benefit. The worker must always be alert to find ways to "save face" for each member, even small children. In most situations, having flare-ups without having a clear goal is not a good idea.

It is your responsibility to make sure that you do not open up old wounds or intense emotional issues unless you have the time and skills to diffuse them and turn them into a positive result. Remember, the major part of family violence is related directly to the intense emotions that family members evoke in each other. The family session is designed to elicit cooperative feelings among the family, not incite negative feelings. Eliciting negative feelings, if pursued, should be a means to something, and should not be the goal.

Case example: Family Session

Sixteen-year-old Michelle had been at the New Beginning, a group home facility for delinquent adolescents, for the past 3 months. The list of problems was long and varied: failure in school, truancy, running away, drug dealing and alcohol abuse, an abortion at age 15, and she was on probation for various delinquent behaviours. After 3 years of trying to cope with her problems, having tried individual and family counselling, group therapy, in-patient psychiatric hospitalisation 3 times, and a transfer to 3 different schools, the mother filed for a Child In Need of Protective Service (CHIPS) petition and refused to take her home. Mother was convinced that she and her second husband were unable to take care of Michelle any longer, and that she had to "save" the rest of the family from destruction.

The case was referred to FBS for an evaluation for a possible return home and on-going treatment if needed, since Michelle began to say that she wanted to go home. Mother was beginning to think that it might work out, based on their several successful week-end visits and Michelle's expressed desire to come home, which was for the first time. Another important factor in considering a return home was the mother's fairly stable recovery from her alcohol abuse.

The family session was held at the group-home facility; Michelle, her mother, and her stepfather were present. The other 2 children were in school and Michelle's biological father was said to have had no contact with the children for years.

Worker:(To mother) So, what have you noticed different about Michelle that gives you the idea that it might work out this time if Michelle returns home?

Mother: She seems to have calmed down more. She is not so crazy about going out on week-ends, she is nicer to other people in the family. Her friends don't call at all hours of the morning. I guess she generally stays put and acts like she wants to be part of the family.

Worker:(To Michelle) Is that right? How are you doing that?

Michelle: It's not that hard. I want to go home now. It's really boring here. I stay in my room a lot. I don't belong here, I should be home.

Worker: I'm curious about what made you decide that you want to go home now?

Michelle: I'm tired of running, tired of getting in trouble, and I decided I want my life to be different.

Worker:(To mother) Is this new for Michelle to say this to you?

Mother: It is really different for her to say that, but I still don't trust that it's going to stay that way.

Worker: Of course, I don't blame you. So, what do you need to see Michelle do that will tell you that things are really different this time and it will work out?

Mother: I know that she is a teenager and don't expect her to be perfect but she has to stop using drugs and stay in school.

Michelle: But I haven't used drugs for 2 months and I'm getting As and Bs in school here.

Worker: You did what? You did all of that by yourself? Gosh, that's quite an accomplishment. Not using drugs for 2 months is a long time. How do you do it?

Michelle: I just don't use it. I just stay away from the kids who use drugs and stay in my room.

Worker: I know it's not hard to get drugs here. When you are stuck in here, its harder to say "no" to drugs. So, how do you do it?

Michelle: Once I make up my mind, it's not hard to do. Last year I didn't use drugs for 6 months.

Worker: How did you do that?

Mother: That's when she was pregnant.

Michelle: When I knew I was pregnant I didn't want to use drugs any more, so I just stopped it.

Worker: That's incredible. You must be a strong person.

Stepfather: She sure can be when she wants to be.

Worker: So, what is Michelle like when she is strong?

Stepfather: She can be a lot of fun. She makes everybody laugh, she is a good-hearted kid inside.

Worker: So, what do you notice about Michelle when she is good-hearted, and when she shows a sense of humour?

Stepfather: She helps everybody. She is very sensitive and gets upset easier than other kids. She has a way of saying things that is really grown-up sometimes.

After continuing with the description of changes Michelle had made, the next step was to describe how other people were participating in the changes; the "ripple effect" of how other changes in the family affect each other. Mother's criteria for Michelle coming home were still that she must a) stay drug free, and b) stay in school. Both were good goals, that is, fairly easy to measure, monitor, and clearly would be good for Michelle.

Worker: Tell me, Michelle, what do you notice different around the house when you are helpful, easy to get along, and fun to be around?

Michelle: Well, mother doesn't yell at me anymore, mom and Tom are getting along better, and it's nice to be home. I don't feel like I have to run away or something.

Worker: Would you say these are the things you noticed since mom stopped drinking or were some of these there before?

Mother: I have to admit I was in pretty bad shape. We fought a lot, and it didn't help the kids. I just couldn't cope with all the problems. It was bad enough that we fought, but Michelle's problem didn't help at all. Sometimes, I'd fight with both of them."

Discussion:

At this point, it would have been easy for the worker to focus on problems since the family members seemed to want to open up the issues. Focusing on the problems usually implies that there is a direct cause; someone is responsible for the problem and someone is at fault.

Worker: So, what will have to be different for all three of you to say that "maybe things will work out this time", that is, for Michelle to stay away from drugs and to stay in school and for you to have things under a reasonable control?

Michelle: Well, I am talking to my P.O. about going to the alternative school and I know some kids at the NA that I used to belong before.

Mother: I know I have to keep going to AA. Maybe Tom and I need some help in how not to get into it in front of the kids.

Discussion:

As you can see from this interchange, clear ideas about what had to be different, who had to do what in order to maintain the change, were emerging. Michelle was already making some plans for school and for how she would stay-drug free. Mother was also realising that she had to do her part by continuing to control her alcohol abuse and that there were some issues in her marriage which needed further work. The next task for all the family members was to find ways to stay on the right track, to increase the successes and to get back on the track if they faltered. The worker's job was to monitor their progress, encourage them, offer various ways to stay on track.

Case example: Helen and Peter

Helen, a 31-year-old single parent of 3 children, aged 12, 10, and 5, came to the attention of the Child Protective Service (third time for this case) because of frequent disappearances, for 2-3 days at a time, when she would go on drinking binges. The most recent episode had been reported by Helen's mother.

Helen had a continuing on and off relationship, with Pete, who had been in trouble with the law for drug possession and dealing, a number of DWI (Driving While Intoxicated) violations, theft, and other legal and alcohol related problems. Pete was the father of Helen's 3 children, not adjudicated, because Helen has consistently claimed that she was too drunk to know who the father was in order to protect Pete from having to pay child support.

Helen met Pete at age 16, and fell madly in love with him. Pete had psychologically abused Helen and often threatened to abandon her. From time to time, Pete had not given her any money for the children, and had several girlfriends "on the side".

The worker asked relationship questions to assess Helen's perception of their relationship, such as:

Worker: What do you suppose Pete would say if he was here and I were to ask him whether you love him more or he loves you more?

Helen: He would say that I love him more than he loves me.

Worker: Who would he say needs the other person more, you need him more, or he needs you more?

Helen: I know he would say that I need him more than he does me.

Worker: On the scale of 1 to 10, 10 means high and 1 means low, what number do you suppose Pete will say he is at for being willing to change?"

Helen: I, uh, I would say he is at 2.

Worker: How much confidence do you have that he will change?

Helen: I would say maybe 1 or 2 at most.

Questions along these lines, scaling questions, helped Helen recognise that she must change first instead of waiting for Pete to become "good", which might never happen.

The case was transferred to FBS about 1 week after the Child Protective Service worker's investigation, which indicated that Helen's binge episodes had become more frequent in recent years. The FBS team decided to take advantage of her remorse and offered service to Helen immediately. Realising how close to losing her children she was, Helen decided to accept the service and that she had to do something about her problem.

Because Helen's relationship with her mother was very close, (both agreed that they talked to each other 5 - 10 times each day), the team decided to evaluate the mother-daughter relationship to assess whether mother was "enabling" Helen's alcohol abuse and also to find out in what ways her family could be a resource for her recovery.

The family session with Helen, her mother Jackie, sister Kelly (8 years younger) and their small children was held at Jackie's house. It indicated that Jackie hated Pete "with a passion", that everyone in the family, repeatedly over the years, had advised Helen to leave Pete, that he was "using her", that he "jerked her around", he would never commit himself to the relationship, and that Helen would be better off leaving him. The session included a touching expression of much caring and closeness, a demonstration of sense of humour, and showed how they were able to laugh and talk about shared good times. All of them shared a cry about the painful reality that Helen's brother is dying of cancer, and it was re-affirmed that Jackie was "right there" whenever Helen needed her.

Helen recognised that Pete was not good for her, but she needed to get her "act together" before anything else, which meant that she needed to control her binge drinking. She was clear that she did not want to "lose the family ties" with her mother and sister, which she came to recognise as very strong.

As this case demonstrates, it is difficult to expect most families to participate in family sessions every time. However, when handled well, family session can have a powerful impact on the client and the family unit as a whole.

CONDUCTING COUPLE SESSIONS

Some people find working with couples difficult and some have a special knack for it and love working with couples. It is by and large a personal preference and depends a great deal on what you feel comfortable with. All FBS cases involve some work with couples, whether the man is involved in the session or not, whether the woman acknowledges that there is a man in her life or not. Some call them invisible men (Franklin-Boyd, 1990) since the majority of women behave as if the man is not there because of various social welfare policies. The child welfare workers also behave as if the man in the client's life does not exist. However, we know from clinical and other experience that the client's relationship with her "man" greatly influences her parenting ability. In FBS, you can expect to see a great many more complex couple relationships than in most clinical practices. Therefore, it is important to have skills to handle couple sessions.

Because of many women clients' secrecy about their liaison with a man, you may encounter a man during a home visit that you did not know was living there. And it is a good idea to be prepared to conduct a couple session spontaneously, taking advantage of the opportunities when presented.

So, why should you do something that is so complex and difficult to do? Simply because the benefit is manifold. When conducted well, the benefit of the couple session to the client and to your work is hard to measure immediately but you will see the long-term benefits in child welfare. When the client feels competent about the important relationships in her life, she is more likely to parent well. When you utilise the existing resources, your work is likely to be easier and the pay-off greater.

WHEN IS A COUPLE SESSION USEFUL?

As you would with the family sessions, you may request a couple session whether the couple are co-habiting or not. The following are signs that a couple session may be helpful.

1. When it is clear that the client's relationship with her partner is creating many problems for her, thus, affecting her ability to parent.
2. When the parent-child problem seems to be aggravated by the presence of a third person, mother's boyfriend or a stepfather.
3. When the client appears overly protective or secretive about her relationship with her man.
4. When the client's relationship with her man appears abusive, or related to drug or alcohol abuse.
5. When the adolescent child of the client becomes protective of his/her mother from her abusive boyfriend, thus creating conflict and at times violent

confrontation which result in some serious consequences.

6. When the mother's extended family rejects the "boyfriend" causing her alienation from her family of origin. This puts her in a vulnerable position, at greater risk of abuse by her man, and in turn her children are exposed to witnessing their mother's abuse.

As you can see, this covers pretty well most of your cases.

WAYS TO INCLUDE THE SPOUSE IN SESSION

Many people regard the "social worker" from the Welfare Department as the "busybody" or "baby snatcher" and try to avoid running into "case workers". Unless they have been "in the system" for various reasons, most men would rather avoid "social workers", including FBS, since they don't quite understand how one is different from the other.

Therefore, including men in the session may be somewhat difficult initially and may require a gentle approach. The following are some helpful techniques.

1. In talking to the client, ask who is most helpful to her, who helps her out the most. Talk about her needing help with raising children as a natural thing, that all mothers need to get away from their children, and that her need for an adult relationship is natural

2. Taking the stance that "it is natural to have a relationship with a man", ask about her social life, how she manages being lonely, who helps her out financially and with children.

3. When she indicates that there is trouble with her "man", ask about his perception of the situation, using the relationship question, such as, "If he were here, and if I were to ask him what it would take for the two of you to get along better, what do you suppose he would say?"

4. More of these questions, (asking what she thinks he thinks about what she thinks) strongly suggests to the client that you value the man's opinion, even though he is absent. They also suggest to her that his view will play an important part in finding solutions.

5. When you let her know that you value his opinion, unlike her family who has no use for him, she is more likely to allow her "boyfriend" to participate in treatment.

6. When you unexpectedly run into the "boyfriend" invite his input with respect and appreciation. Focusing on finding "solutions" to their differences that cause difficulties bypasses the issue of blame, thus enabling them to move on to more constructive tasks.

MATTER OF NEUTRALITY

As mentioned in the previous section on conducting a family session, maintaining neutrality is crucial to successful outcome in all cases. However, in the couple session, neutrality (that is not taking sides with either party in a dyad) is more difficult since many couple relationships reflect some aspect of the worker's own personal relationships.

When you find yourself taking sides, or even leaning towards thinking that one or the other side in a dyad is "more right" or "more at fault", always try to keep in mind the "flip side" of one's point of view. Nothing happens in a vacuum and personal relationships are systemic; that is, there cannot be clear cause and effect. Thus, whatever the problem, both sides are "causes" and "victims" of their perceptions and therefore, they try doing "more of the same" things that do not work. Again, avoid doing what everyone else tried and failed.

WORKING WITH ONE PARTNER

Since relationships are made up of predictable, repetitive action-reaction patterns that occur over time, even when you have only one partner who is willing to work on solving the relationship issues, there is still much you can do. Just make sure that you use the assessment outlined in this book and go over it again, targeting the solution finding. When one person makes changes, the other has to react to them, thus disrupting the dysfunctional patterns of interactions.

CONFLICTING GOALS

Workers are apt to come across couples who have conflicting goals for their relationship, that is, she wants to make it work, while he wants to leave, or is taking steps to do so.

The initial important component in assessment of a couple's relationship is to figure out how much "goodwill" or positive regard and affection there is between the couple. When you get a feeling that the couple really like each other, and there is general positive regard for each other, then any disagreement between them can be reframed as two approaches to the same goal.

Example:

His wife "kicked him out because he refuses to shape up, get a job, carry his share of the responsibility". It can be framed as her way of letting him know that she values the relationship so much that she is insisting on his becoming a man that she can respect.

Case example: Leroy and Lucinda

Leroy (aged 26) and Lucinda (aged 27) had been together for about 3 years, and had been married for about a year; Lucinda had a 7-year-old child from her previous relationship. They reported that they used to be physically abusive to each other but somehow learned to stop that. Instead they screamed, yelled, and argued, so loud that they had been evicted once and were concerned about another eviction. After about a year of working for a temporary job service, Leroy finally got a permanent job which he wanted to keep badly. The issue had to do with Leroy's suspicion that Lucinda was "fooling around" when she went out with her girlfriends. Lucinda denied this.

The couple said they loved each other and both wanted to make the marriage work. From various signs, it was clear that they did love each other and were greatly pained by the fights. When asked who would be willing to go first to make things better, Leroy volunteered that he would take the first step (which the worker would suggest) to make things better between them. Lucinda promised that she would take the second step. The worker decided to positively use the couple's competitive style of relating to each other.

The worker gave the following message and suggestion:

"It is very clear to us (the FBS team) that Lucinda is a very strong-willed person and it takes a strong man to love a strong woman. We can see you two are a good match and can make this marriage work, even though it will take lots of hard work. It is clear to us that Leroy is terribly important to Lucinda, since what Leroy does or does not do, says or does not say, has such an impact on her. And the same goes for Leroy. What Lucinda does or does not say, or do, has such an impact on Leroy (heads nodding). You both are very sensitive about each other and both of you want to be loved and cared about by the other person equally.

"By the way, we like the way Leroy took the leadership position by volunteering to go first to improve things, but it is clear to us that both of you are capable of going first. We suggest that whoever decides to take the first step does the following: any time you sense the other person is upset, down, unsure about trusting, we want you to give the other person a squeeze of a hand, a hug, or a pat on the back without words. The other person's job is to take the second step by responding in a similar way. When we return next time, tell us what difference this makes."

Discussion:

The workers used several techniques with Leroy and Lucinda:

1. Reframing.

It was clear to the team that Lucinda was no "push over", she was a strong, articulate, vocal woman who could easily intimidate most men. Leroy, on the other hand, though quiet and soft spoken, did not easily back down. The team decided to reframe their positions as coming from strengths, rather than see them as problems. Their tendencies to fight about everything, to correct, and to counter everything with their own reasoning was reframed as a sign of caring and valuing the other person's opinion.

2. Using Existing Strengths

Even though Leroy volunteered to "go first", the workers decided to use their tendency to be competitive and told them that either could "go first", thus increasing their desire to do something to improve.

3. Do Something Different Task

Since their tendency to argue verbally got them into trouble, the team decided to go for non-verbal ways to communicate their positive feelings for each other.

4. Observation Task
The last task was for them to tell the team what difference this made, thus the couple was directed to look for something "different". When they looked for it, they would be more likely to find it.

CONCLUSION
This chapter has described conducting family and couple sessions in detail so that the FBS worker can be introduced to the subtle techniques for finding strengths and encouraging clients to see themselves as having successes and resources. As mentioned earlier, conducting effective family and couple sessions takes some practice and requires clear directions, but when conducted well, the sessions can be very productive for the family.

Eight
MIDDLE PHASE AND TERMINATION

A. ONGOING EVALUATION
Now that you have initiated some activities, the next step is to evaluate the assessment and revise it if necessary Any additional information that was not available during the initial assessment phase may shed different light on the case. Since treatment is a constantly changing, fluid, evolving process, the worker needs to be alert to refining the goal and evaluating progress. New information not only adds to the refinement of the assessment but also alerts the worker to any change in direction.

Evaluation is not carried out just at the time of termination but is an on-going, constant process, and therefore, gives directions as to how you should modify and revise your goals and strategies as you go along. A good, on-going evaluation means that there should not be any surprises at the time of termination.

The following criteria will be useful to keep in mind during the middle phase of treatment.

1. Each contact with the client becomes an evaluative session. Pay close attention to how new information you may have confirms what you are doing or gives new ideas about what to do or not to do.
2. Clients do not know what kind of information the worker is looking for or what will be helpful to the worker. Therefore, think of any new information you receive as adding to the larger picture, not necessarily as something they were trying to hide.
3. Some new information is useful and some not. The guide to sorting out what is useful and what is not, depends on what your treatment goal is. Does this new information provide you with better ideas on how to achieve the goal for this family? Does it give you new ideas about who will be most interested in doing something about the problem?
4. Be flexible and willing to change your mind in the light of new information. It takes confidence in your ability and trust in your own intuitive and common sense judgment to acknowledge your mistake and revise your initial impression about the goals and targets of intervention.
5. Keep the following questions in mind:
   a) Is the initial goal appropriate?
   b) Am I working with the right person?
   c) How close is the client to achieving the goal?
   d) What would be the next sign of success?
   e) Who has to do what, when and how to take the next step towards the goal?
   f) What needs to be revised? What can stay the same?

6. What are the signs of lack of progress?. If you find yourself feeling frustrated with a case or feeling like you are working harder than the client, you may have reached an impasse. No need to panic. There are some steps to take to remedy this.

   a) Do not blame or get angry at the client. It probably is neither your fault, nor your client's. The client may be just as frustrated as you are. So, both of you are in it together.

   b) Mention to the client that things are not going well and that you may have made a mistake. When you involve the client in making things right, they will become more motivated to work with you. It is not all your work. Remember, clients are like anybody else and people are willing to help those in trouble when asked. It is empowering for the client to be allowed to discover the helpful, cooperative, and nurturing side of herself.

   c) Review your goals. Was the goal too big? Start with a small, simple one. Is the right person involved in finding solutions? What is the sign of success for the new goal?

B. OFFERING SUGGESTIONS AND TASKS

FBS workers are 1in an excellent position to find solutions to clients' problems, not only because they are trained, but simply because they are in a position to stand back and observe the patterns of "more of the same" that clients tend to repeat.

A good way to explain this to yourself is that the clients are in the middle of a picture when they try to solve their problem. When someone is a part of a picture, it is difficult for that person to see the whole picture. But as an outsider, the worker can see the whole picture.

Since it is easier to see the whole picture, workers can easily make the mistake of offering suggestions and advice too soon, thus becoming impatient with the client. This phenomenon can be described as "being ahead of a client". Remember, as a worker, you have an influence on the client to a point. Knowing how to pace the client's readiness to change is a skill that comes with training and experience.

There follow some guidelines for maximising your influence on the client so that the likelihood of client compliance with your suggestion is increased.

THE TASK HAS TO MAKE SENSE TO THE CLIENT

Even the best suggestion that the worker makes is useless if the client does not follow it. Frequently, workers blame the client, and become frustrated and angry with her. It might make the worker feel better for a few minutes but still the task is to help the client to follow the suggestion and "Do Something Different". So, how do you get the client to "do something different", since everybody, including clients, do things in a certain way because that way seems the most sensible at the time?

Before making your suggestion to your client, review it and see if you think your client will accept your suggestion as a sensible thing to do from her point of view.

When you can say "yes" to yourself, then the likelihood of the client accepting your suggestion will increase.

WHAT TO DO

1. Be patient. Do not jump into offering advice or suggestions. Take some time to study the situation, ask questions that the client did not think of asking herself. (See Chapters 5 and 6 on interviewing.) Listen attentively first.
2. Challenge the client's conception of the problem. Gently start to introduce some doubt into the way the client conceptualises the problem. The client's way of thinking about the problem is not helping her find solutions.

Case example 1

Client: You know, the reason Tyrone talks back to me is because he hates me. I can just see the hatred in his eyes and the stuff he says. I didn't teach him that way. I always tell him he has to respect his mother. I am his mother and he can't talk to me that way.

Discussion:

The worker has several options for his response Since the mother is more upset about her son's behaviour than the son is, the mother is most likely to become a "customer" for change. As long as the mother sees the son's behaviour as "hatred" towards her, she will respond accordingly. If she saw the same behaviour as something other than "hatred", the chances of her changing her interaction with her son will increase. The worker can respond to this by introducing some doubt into this mother's way of thinking.

Worker: You think so? From what you said about Tyrone so far, it seems a little different from most boys hating their mothers. It just doesn't sound the same to me. You know, I work with lots of children his age. And I met him and talked to him quite a bit. He is not like most kids

Client: So, what do you think it is?

Discussion:

If the client has come this far, that is, she becomes curious about your way of thinking about her son, the chances of her wanting to hear your ideas about her difficulty with her son will be increased. Most parents want to believe their children are different from other kids. All parents want their children to do better in life than they have done themselves.

Worker: It seems more like he wants to flex his muscles a little bit. It is clear that you have taught him all the right values. I guess now he needs to test what he has learned."

Discussion:

Make sure the client is ready to hear your ideas. Working with people calls for a sensitivity to "timing". A suggestion offered at the wrong time, that is, when the client is not ready to "hear", will fall on "deaf ears". This is the major complaint from parents about their pre-adolescent and teenage children, and workers don't need to repeat what the parents do.

You will know that the clients are ready to hear you when they are asking your opinion on better ideas or different ways to solve problems. (See chapter 2 on assessment of the customer-type client.)

Positively frame what the client is doing and give her lots of positive feedback about her past and current successes. You can always suggest that what the client is doing is her way of trying to "improve her life", "to improve the children's lives", to "make things better", and so on. The client's motives are always for the good of the others and herself.

State the suggestion you are making as the natural next step to complete the job she started, or as the next step in making her tasks a little bit easier.

Case example 2

A mother bitterly complains about her 14-year-old daughter, Cindy, who is failing in school, is late getting to school, plays truant now and then, and runs away when her mother is trying to reprimand her. The mother's view is that she has absolutely failed to bring her daughter up properly because now she feels that she is losing control of her, and that Cindy's "wild" behaviour is caused by the "wrong friends she hangs out with".

A session with the daughter indicates that she feels helpless about her situation, gets very upset that her mother calls her "names", feels that "nobody cares" about her, is afraid of getting "hit on the head", and is ashamed of failing while her younger sister is doing better. Cindy acts "street smart" but at times acts younger than her age, and wants some reassurance and structure from adults.

When the mother's problem solving methods were examined closely, it became apparent that the mother needed to stop "yelling and screaming" at Cindy, to be more positive with her, to make it possible for Cindy to approach her and to help her realise how much her mother loves her and cares about her welfare. Clearly the daughter needed to make some changes also, such as, staying in school, getting some help with her academic deficiency, carefully selecting friends, and finding ways to get along with her family.

Discussion:

It is going to be important right from the beginning not to be too much ahead of the client and indeed to introduce some doubt into the mother's view of the problem so that she can feel some control over the situation. Viewing the problem as being Cindy's "bad friends" is not very useful since the mother cannot select friends for Cindy. Parents generally cannot select friends for children of Cindy's age, and whatever friends Cindy chooses, she has to believe are of her own choice. The mother needs to help Cindy to learn to use her own judgement and to make good decisions. How might this be done, and how might you frame positively what mother is doing?

Supposing the client is ready, ask yourself what kind of tasks it would be appropriate to set for both mother and daughter, which will move them towards their goal.

THE WORKER'S TASK

1. Ask about any time mother and Cindy get along. Can they do it again? If yes, suggest it as a task. If no, ask the "miracle question" to get some ideas.
2. Ask about when Cindy behaves within an acceptable range. Find out what it would take for Cindy to repeat this behaviour.
3. Was there any time when Cindy did well in school? What would it take for her to do it again?
4. Assess who is most interested in finding solutions. Work with that person closely. Elicit others' help.
5. What is important to that person and make sure you connect with that person.
6. Find out everybody's strengths and resources. Use them.
7. Find out who tried what, and how that did not work. Rule these out.
8. Establish a small, realistic, and measurable goal.
9. List the family's past successes and accomplishments.
10. Present the task as the next step in completing their on-going aspiration to improve their lives.
11. Make sure the task makes sense to the client.

WHAT TO DO IF THE CLIENT DOES NOT FOLLOW SUGGESTIONS

First of all, do not panic and do not get upset with the client. When she fails to carry out the suggestions you make, there usually is a good reason for it from the client's point of view. The following steps may be a useful guide to reviewing the situation.

1. Find out from the client what she did instead. Find out all you can about what she found useful or helpful in doing what she did instead of following your suggestion.
2. If she did not do anything, find out if the problem is better. If it is better, find out what she did to make it better. The client may have a better solution than you have. Be open minded about it.
3. If the client did not do the task and says the problem is not better, you may have the wrong goal or the wrong person to work with. Review your goal and who the "customer" is. The client may become a "customer" for her own goal.
5. If you have the wrong "customer" or wrong goal, start over and proceed with the appropriate steps.
6. Let the client know that she used her good judgment for not following your suggestion and compliment her on using her own judgment.
7. Then ask the client what she believes she needs to do to solve the problem.
8. Emphasise the gravity and the seriousness of the problem.

9. Maintain the attitude and posture that the client knows what is best for her and her family.

C. WHAT TO DO IF THERE IS NO PROGRESS

If you know you are not making any progress, that is, you are becoming frustrated, you feel like you are working harder than the client, you say things like "It's like pulling teeth", "It's like hitting the brick wall", "I wonder what I'm doing here", or have similar thoughts, you are probably right to wonder what is going on. Do not dismiss these nagging doubts in your mind. They are good clues which you should not ignore.

All counsellors, family therapists, FBS workers, Child Protective Service workers and everyone who deals with people problems, face these doubts from time to time. It is quite normal and does not mean that you made a mistake or that something is wrong with you. The important thing is to pay attention to these clues and do something about it.

So, what to do? Review the chapter and sections that deal with impasse and client non-compliance. Just start over and make sure that you get some form of consultation from your team, colleagues, supervisors, or consultant.

D. ENHANCING POSITIVE CHANGES

Once you can see that the client is starting to make some positive changes, the easiest and most enjoyable part of your job begins. The next step is to enhance changes and continue to improve on the gains that the client is making.

AS YOU MOVE CLOSER TO THE END

Think of yourself as a coach and a consultant to your clients at this point. Both roles have elements of teaching, nurturing, encouraging, healing, cheerleading, suggesting, and molding your client's opinion about her ability and skills, while occasionally insisting that things be done in certain ways. But all good coaches know that influencing self-perception and improving self-esteem have the greatest impact on performance.

Here follows a list of tasks you need to do after the initial contacts and as you begin to see some positive changes.

1. Clients often do not notice their own successes. Look for even a small change, something you notice different about her and comment on it. It may be something as small as noticing that the dishes are cleared away, she is wearing some make-up, she has combed her hair, she went to church, made contact with an old friend, the children are smiling and acting their age appropriately, the snow is shovelled, the grass is cut, and so on.
2. Look for something new to comment on and encourage during each contact you make. Clients may not be aware of these little signs of successes. With enough

repetition, they may learn to do it themselves, given time and recognition.

3. Find out what you are doing that works. However small, ordinary, or simple, keep noticing what you do that works with a particular client or with FBS clients in general. Know your repertoire of things you do well with clients, things that work for you. Remember to use those skills when you need to.

4. A good coach gives constant feedback. Your positive feedback will help the client recognise what strengths she has and what is different in her life. These are the things she can do for herself when you terminate the case. Unless the client knows what changes she is making, and therefore, what is different in her life, she will not know how to transfer her learning to other situations.

E. BEFORE YOU MOVE ON TO A NEW PROBLEM

Once the problem initially agreed on becomes less of a concern and fades into the background, clients and workers are often eager to move on to tackle the next set of issues.

It is easy to move on to the next set of problems without having a breathing space to realise the full impact of success. Make sure that you take some time out to relish and enjoy the positive changes, and of course, give credit to the client for all the positive things she has done to bring about the changes.

1. Find out in step-by-step fashion what is better with the original problem: who is doing what, when, how, with what results. This is useful information.

2. Do not let the client move on to the next set of problems. Reassure the client that you will return to her concerns later but stick to your agenda of making sure she understands what she is doing that is different and that is linked to success.

3. Find out what the client learned from the successes.

4. Find out what the client can remember to do next time if the problem comes up again.

F. IF THE CLIENT REPORTS THINGS ARE WORSE

Frequently the clients will start the next session with "Nothing is better", or "Things are worse" as the opening comment.

1. Do not become discouraged. Behave as if you expected it, since it is really quite natural for life to have a rhythm of ups and downs.

2. Ask in what way things are worse. Start to introduce some doubt into the client's perception of how much worse things are.

3. If it is a new problem, do not hesitate to set that aside and return to the original problem that you both agreed to work on.

4. If it is the same problem that you had both agreed to work on, ask about the details of how, what, when, with whom, and in what ways, things are worse.

5. Start pointing out some difference you notice and start to give the client credit for having made some small changes.

6. Ask questions like "How did you think of doing it that way?" or "Where did you come up with that idea?" or "That's great! Whose idea was it that you do it that way?"
7. Some clients report that nothing is better even though in reality you can see the positive changes, such as, her voice is stronger, she is more active, the children are behaving better, and so on. Go back and review whether you have a "visitor" or a "complainant" - you may not have a "customer" yet. If this is the case, start over and make sure that you are working with a "customer".

G. TERMINATION
TWO DIFFERENT WAYS TO TERMINATE A CASE
Termination of a case starts at the beginning of a case and ends when the case ends. In between these two points, there is continuous and on-going evaluation as to how close you are to achieving the goals.

There are two different ways of determining when the joint work between therapist and client has been achieved: lapse of time or goal accomplishment.

TIME AS AN EXTERNAL CRITERION FOR TERMINATION
Most frequently used by the brief psychodynamic treatment models, and utilised by insurance companies or Health Maintenance Organisation (HMO), or Employee Assistance Program (EAP), this approach uses the number of sessions as the criterion for when to end contact. Clearly such an approach has both a positive and negative effect on the therapeutic outcome.

Mann uses 12 sessions maximum limit (Mann, 1973), while Sifneos limits to 8 – 14 sessions (Sifneos 1985), and Malan up to 40 sessions. However, all have stringent patient selection criteria as developed by Sifneos (1965) and agreed by Mann (1973) that patients must :
a) Be above average intelligence,
b) Have at least one meaningful relationship with another person,
c) Be in emotional crisis,
d) Have the ability to express feelings and interact with the therapist,
e) Be motivated to work hard during psychotherapy,
f) Have a specific complaint.

It is not difficult to see the limitations of this approach; the stringent client selection criteria are difficult to enforce when working in the public sector, such as FBS, and even in some private, voluntary sectors, such as community mental health clinics or community agencies that are supported by public funds, and therefore, must service everyone who walks into the clinic.

The problem with using time as the main criterion is that some clients can "just buy time" with passive-aggressive attitudes, waiting out the designated period.

Many FBS models determine a specific number of days, such as 30 , 45 or 90 days, in order to determine how long a case will stay open. Usually, at the end of the specified number of days the case is either transferred to other on-going programs or closed. This approach can be useful since clients will know exactly when the end is coming. Knowing that there is a distinct end to the contact can help to keep both the client and the worker motivated. It can also be helpful in pacing, monitoring the progress, and generally by keeping track of number of days left to accomplish certain goals. It also forces the client and worker to be concise and limit the treatment goal to a manageable level. Keeping track of a number of days is simpler and easier to manage than the approach outlined in the following section.

Even when you are using the number of days as a way of deciding on termination, it is a good idea to frequently remind clients of their accomplishments and the achievement of their goals.

GOAL ACHIEVEMENT AS CRITERIA

Some treatment models, such as the Mental Research Institute (MRI) model of brief therapy (Watzlawick, Fishe, and Weakland, 1975), use specific goal accomplishment as a criterion for termination. If the goal is achieved before the 10 sessions or 90 days deadline, for example, the case can be closed. When the goal is described in behavioural, concrete, measurable terms, it is easy to see when to terminate. In other words, the sooner the client accomplishes her goals, the sooner the contacts with the therapist can end. Often this is a powerful motivator for the client.

The difficulty with using goal attainment as a criterion is that some goals, even after having been achieved, take some time to test. For example, some problems such as occasional depressive episodes, infrequent fighting between a couple, violence, or drinking binges, etc., do not have a frequent pattern. If the drinking, loss of temper, fights that get out of control or suicide gestures, and so on, occur under extremely stressful life circumstances and are not frequent occurrences with a predictable pattern, a good test of time would be necessary to know if enough of a solid solution pattern has been accomplished. These situations will obviously be discussed and rehearsed with the client before termination but still it is a matter of "a judgment call."

Whatever criteria you use in your own mind, it is again important to know when the contact should end. I suggest that you review the guideline for establishing treatment goals.

REVIEW OF INITIAL AND REVISED GOALS

As time goes on, you need to keep track of the initial goals agreed on between you and the client. It is useful for the therapist to review those with the client regularly, using scaling questions. Not only do you need to ask the client these questions but you also need to ask yourself to decide how close you are to achieving your goals.

Examples of scaling questions:

Worker: I want to ask you a slightly different question. Looking back, suppose when we first started that your life was at 1 and where you want your life to be at is 10, where would you say you are at today between 1 and 10?

Client: I would say I am at maybe 4 or 5.

Worker: What do you suppose it will take for you to be at maybe 5 or 6?
or

Worker: When you reach 5 or 6, what do you suppose will be different with you (or what will you be doing that you are not doing now?)

Worker: On the same scale, 10 means you have every confidence that you will continue to control your drug use, 1 means you have no confidence at all, where would you say you are at today?

Client : I would guess at 4 because I still get cravings and I still get crabby with the kids.

Worker: So, what (or how long) would it take you to move up from 4 to 5?

Client: I have to keep going to AA and keep busy.

Worker: Suppose your mother was here and I were to ask her, what do you suppose she would say she needs to see you do for her to say that you are at 5?

ASSESSING THE READINESS FOR TERMINATION

Worker: You have made a lots of changes since we started to work together. On a scale of 1 to 10, with 10 meaning you have every confidence that you will stay at 5 and 1 meaning you have no confidence at all, where would you put yourself between 1 and 10 today?

Client: I would say I am at 7.

Worker: I think it takes some getting used to the changes you have made. What would it take for you to stay at 7 for the next month? Two months?

Client: I will just have to keep doing what I've been doing.

Worker: If your mother (or someone else) were here and I were to ask her, what do you suppose she would say you need to do to stay at 7?

Client: She would probably say that I will have to keep going to the NA, keep busy, stay away from my drug using friends, stay away from James, stay in touch with her, and things like that.

Asking the client about her confidence in maintaining change gives a good indication of how integrated into her life the client sees the new behaviour as being, and very often offers her the opportunity of specifying clearly what she is doing and needs to continue doing to maintain the change. The more concretely these behaviours are described, and the higher the client's confidence in the changes made, the more confident the worker can be.

DISCUSSION OF SETBACK

Worker: What would be the earliest sign to you that you are starting to slide back?"
or "What would your family notice about you that would tell them that you are beginning to slide backward?

Client: I will get moody, not see anyone, not go out, get depressed.

Worker: They sound to me like signs that you have started to slide back. Do you know what comes even before that? What do you have to do so that you can catch yourself before you start to slide back?

You can repeat variations of this kind of discussion as often as you think necessary. These questions imply that the client must take responsibility for monitoring herself, which is an empowering message. It says to the client that you not only trust her to look after her own best interest but also that it is her responsibility to do so. These are the tools she will need to work with after contact with you is terminated.

A minor setback or relapse is to be expected. Look at the setback as a "test before graduation", or look at it as an opportunity to learn something new about her ability to handle tough life situations. The setback may be because of the client "having forgotten what to do", or be "a reminder of what she needs to remember to do".

When the client has actually suffered a setback, review the event with the client, and emphasise what she has learned from the episode. The experience can be used to plan how she is going to handle a similar situation differently, should it arise again. For example, should grandmother criticise mother again, how will she handle it differently so that she does not take it out on her children?

HOW CLOSE ARE YOU TO ACHIEVING THE GOALS?

As you continue to evaluate the progress towards goal achievement, you need to keep an eye on the accomplishments of the client. Since this is a joint activity, clients need to know what they have achieved and what more they need to do to achieve the goal.

Again, it is important to amplify client success, however small or minor it may seem. For the client it may be the first time she has accomplished something she set out to do and finished it with a positive feeling about it. Therefore, it is crucial for you and the client to jointly evaluate how far she has come and how hard she worked at it. Clients rarely hear compliments or get "a pat on the back" from the people they feel close to, co-workers, relatives, schools, other helpful people in their lives, or even themselves. Wanting to be positively regarded is part of human nature.

WHEN AND HOW TO INITIATE TERMINATION

Again, a limited number of sessions can be a good way to decide when to terminate, but a more helpful way is to review the goals and keep reminding yourself and the client of how far she has come:

1. How does the client understand what she did to find solutions to her problem? Does she have a clear sense of what she did to help herself?
2. Is it the kind of information that can be applied to other situations?
3. Does she have clear ideas on what may be the early signs that things have

started to deteriorate? Does she know what to do if it were to happen?

When you are reasonably sure of positive answers to these questions, then you need to go over these points with the client. The process of termination is also continuous and on-going.

WHAT HAPPENS WHEN YOU ARE NOT SUCCESSFUL WITH A CASE

A valid reason for termination may be when there is no movement in a case. Instead of continuing to do "more of the same" of something that doesn't work, the therapist may consider the following:

1. At the earliest indication that a case is not going well, a consultation with the team or supervisor, or an outside consultant may be called for.
2. When the worker feels that he has exhausted all possible approaches and feels at an impasse, a transfer of the case to another team or another therapist may be useful.

   Reaching an impasse is not always the client's fault, or the worker's. And it does not always mean that the problem is too big, or that the resources are limited or that there is no hope. Thinking about a transfer to another therapist or a consultation sometimes opens up a whole new way of looking at the case and new ideas can emerge. Don't overlook this possibility.
3. Mismatch of worker-client can happen at any time and in any program. Such occurrences are common in the field of psychotherapy and it is unethical to pretend that bad "chemistry" does not exist.

SUCCESSFUL TERMINATION

Life is full of problems to be solved and your clients are no different from anyone else. If you wait until all the client's problems are solved, it could be endless. Many "open" cases are those that workers believe may "blow up", and therefore, for safety reasons, cases are frequently kept open much longer than necessary.

What is important to keep in mind is that "empowering clients" means equipping clients with the tools to solve their own problems as far as possible. When they can't do it on their own, they need to know when to ask for help and where to go for help. Termination can occur when you are confident that the client will know when and where to go to seek help, and not when you are confident that she will never have problems. There is no such thing as a problem-free life. Remember: "life is just one damned thing after another."

OPEN-ENDED TERMINATION

This can occur when there is sufficient change from the treatment point of view but the court's mandate is that the family maintain contact with the DSS for a much longer period. In such situations, these cases may need to be referred to an on-going worker and monitored periodically, or kept on a once a month check-in, or on an "as needed" basis.

Nine
DO SOMETHING DIFFERENT

Most FBS workers will find the procedures outlined in this book useful when followed in a step-by-step fashion. The procedures are based on the first two rules of Solution Focused Therapy which are: Rule 1 - If it ain't broke, don't fix it; Rule 2 - Once you know what works, do more of it. (See Chapter 1.) Now is the time to discuss Rule 3 - If it doesn't work, don't do it again; do something different. This chapter will deal with how to do something different.

WHAT ARE THE SIGNS THAT SOMETHING DIFFERENT NEEDS TO BE DONE?

1. There are cases where it is clear to the worker that doing "more of the same" is not sufficient, and therefore a drastically new behaviour or new pattern of interaction is called for.
2. Even though there are clearly "exceptions" to the problem, the client is not ready to acknowledge them as such.
3. No matter how hard you try to uncover exceptions, there seem to be none.
4. The imagined solution to the problem (miracle picture) appears to call for a new pattern of behaviour for the client.
5. The client is clearly a "customer" and is willing to solve problems, but only if the worker can come up with some creative and innovative ideas of what to do.

There follows a list of 15 common, easy-to-carry-out interventions and suggestions that fall under the generic category of "doing something different". Individualising these to fit each client with their unique sets of circumstances, problems, and strengths, is the worker's job. Keep in mind that these do not apply to all cases or to every client. Matching the client's situation to an appropriate task takes lots of practice. Workers can take the basic principles of various interventions described here, and adapt them to fit the unique situations of each family.

The selection of tasks and interventions is based on a belief that the worker should try the simplest, easiest, and most conservative approach first before trying something more elaborate.

The following interventions are grouped according to with whom they can best be used, clients who are "visitors", "complainants", or "customers". When workers master these interventions, they will find them to be useful in the majority of DSS and FBS cases.

The following 4 interventions can be helpfully used with "visitor", "complainant", and "customer" type clients.

1. COMPLIMENTS

Complimenting is a powerful technique that can be tried before anything else. Compliments alone can be a powerful intervention when you have a "visitor" or are in the early phase of contacts with FBS cases. Do not underestimate their usefulness. As one abusive, violent, volatile, blue collar man in his late '40's said, "honey works better than vinegar". (Of course the worker complimented him on his having gained "the wisdom of life".)

So, what do you want to compliment the client on? It may not necessarily be related to the problem that brought her to the attention of FBS. Anything you notice about the client - the way she makes an effort to look nice, the way she handles her child, cleans her house, maintains a supportive social network anything that you think will help enhance her self-esteem and feeling of competency will help. A colleague described this activity of looking for something to compliment the client on as "holding up a magnifying glass and picking out with a tweezers".* When the client feels better, she will eventually be able to do other positive things for herself and her children. Clients are not aware of what they routinely do; they need feedback about their successes, especially from professionals.

When you cannot think of anything else to suggest to the client, remember to compliment them, especially if you get a sense that most of the client's experience with various professionals has been negative.

Clients can learn to use this approach with their own children or teachers, relatives and other important people in their lives. It even works well among family members. Workers can coach the client on using compliments with others who have influence in her life; help her to watch for positive things that other people are doing and help her start to point these things out to them. Clients will see the results almost immediately.

2. INTRA-SESSION CONSULTATION

Some years ago, I met an In-Home Treatment Team in rural France who carry their portable video camera equipment on their backs when they visit families in remote mountains. Similar work is done in rural Iowa. They set up the video camera in the family's living room and conduct the session. Towards the end of the session, the team members have a brief consultation amongst themselves and ask the family's permission to use the kitchen as their consultation room.

So, why do they do this? For those of you who have not tried such intra-session consultation, either with a team or by yourself, I strongly recommend this practice as a way to increase your effectiveness. It is helpful in enhancing the worker's objectivity and in increasing the impact of the session on the family.

So, how does this work? During the face-to-face interaction with the clients, especially if there is more than one member of the family present, it is not an easy task for the worker to keep track of all the activities that occur in his interaction with the client. However, when there is a physical distance from the family, it becomes somewhat easier to maintain objectivity about the interactional patterns. Since it gives the worker a break from continuous interaction with the client, it

---

* Scott Miller, PhD, Brief Family Therapy Center

allows him some room to review the process of the session and evaluate what has taken place. It simply allows the worker some time to "collect" his thoughts, and summarise his impressions.

Such practice seems also to heighten client expectation and curiosity about what the worker's feedback will be. Everyone wants to hear about themselves and clients are no exception to this. Thus, the worker may notice that the clients change their postures, sit up straight, become more attentive, concentrate on what the worker says, thus heightening the intensity of the session.

So, how should this be handled? The worker, whether working alone or with a team, can explain the procedure during the initial contacts with the client. The explanation may go like this:

"I want to explain to you about what you can expect to happen. I would like to spend about 45 minutes or so talking with you about how I/we can be of help to you. Towards the end of the session, I will take some time out and sit in the next room for about 10 minutes or so and go over all the things that we have discussed. Then I will come back to give you some feedback on what I think might be helpful to you."

A third reason for using this technique is that it allows the worker to assess how closely he is "joining" with the client. There will be an immediate feedback on client agreement or disagreement with the worker's feedback. A good "joining" with the client will produce what Milton Erickson calls "a yes set", nodding or some other indication that the client is in agreement with the worker. This is a good way to pace with the client.

3. NORMALISING

Most workers use this technique quite frequently and perhaps without having given a name to it. Sometimes it is called "universalising". It is a technique of reassuring clients that what they are doing is within the range of normal human behaviour, given their difficult circumstances. It is designed to reassure clients that their feelings, thoughts, and behaviour do not mean that they are "mental", "crazy" or "off the wall", but fall within the normal range of human reactions.

Case example

A young woman came to the attention of FBS because her 4-year-old son "drove her crazy". The young mother's "fiance" died of "Hodgkin's disease" about 3 months prior to the contact, following 4 years of living together. The last 2 years of their life had been very difficult for all of them as the man's illness became more serious and he required a great deal of care. She had an 8-month-old child from this relationship. The 4-year-old son, from another relationship, became restless, more demanding, regressed to more infantile behaviours, and generally drove her "crazy" with his behaviour, in which she saw signs of him being a hyperactive child with attention deficit disorder.

The young mother kept wondering what she was doing wrong, what she was doing that caused her son to misbehave more in recent months. She kept complaining of her lack of energy, feeling that she just couldn't get things done and she found herself "losing it" with the child. She had slapped him too hard, which scared her, since this kind of behaviour was out of character for her. The 4-year-old had always been active, curious, and hard to control, but somehow she had felt less effective with him in recent months.

The worker normalised her depression and her feeling of being overwhelmed. Many things were going on in her life at that time and she needed to grieve and mourn the loss of a lover; to adjust to being a single parent with 2 small children; to cope with a son who required an inordinate amount of structure and attention; and cope with the pressure and complaints from her baby-sitter who threatened to quit because of the 4-year-old child's inability to follow directions.

The worker went a step further than just normalising and told her that it was actually amazing that things were not worse, given the very difficult circumstances in the midst of many changes. What she needed was to allow herself to grieve, to give herself time to heal from the loss, and to gradually regain her previous level of competence.

Another way to normalise the client's concerns is to explain the client's problem as "stress" or reaction to "trauma". These are more hopeful, positive, and less damaging ways to help clients to view themselves. Everyone overcomes stress, and there are things the client can do to manage it. Trauma implies that the difficulty is external to the client, thus giving her hope that she can handle it and overcome it.

Another simple but effective example of normalising is when mothers tell their small children that they are "tired", instead of "naughty". "Tired" implies that it is temporary and will go away when the child gets sufficient amount of rest or sleep. Many mothers report that this approach works well.

Case example: Three Is a Crowd

Mr. and Mrs. P, an interracial couple, came to the attention of the FBS program when Mrs P's 13-year-old daughter from her previous marriage got into a fist fight with her stepfather.

The couple's 2-year-old marriage was full of conflicts over various issues such as: how to discipline Mrs. P's two children; should Mr. P be the "authority" in the home; who should clean the house, do the dishes; how much free time Mrs. P should have as her own; what kind of food they should buy and cook.

The couple fought frequently, accused each other of not caring, not respecting, and at times wondered if they were going to make it as a couple and a family. At times they questioned whether they did the right thing by getting married. Yet, both felt committed to making the marriage work since "deep down inside" they still cared about each other.

The team decided to see their problem from a developmental perspective and complimented the couple for "hanging in there" and trying to make it work. The team told the couple "We can easily see how overwhelming and hopeless it all seems to you at times. Well, no wonder. Most couples usually have some time to 'become a couple', that is, time to work out the nitty-gritty of living with someone else in the same house. Just becoming a couple is itself a hard work. Yet, you started your marriage trying to learn to parent together while at the same time trying to learn to be a couple. No wonder you are so tired, feel overwhelmed, and irritable at times. Anybody would be in your situation." The team was, in fact, amazed that things were not worse than they were.

4. ILLUSION OF CHOICE

Everyone likes to make choices, or, at least wants to believe that they are making choices. When working with FBS clients, presenting an illusion of choice can enable agreement, through the experience of exercising choice, to an option that the client may well find unpalatable, and otherwise may have found unacceptable.

Examples:

Worker: Would it be easier for you to have us visit you at 8 a.m. or at 11 a.m.? (or, Tuesday or Thursday?)

or

Do you want to work on staying sober first or do you want to work on not getting depressed first?

or

Do you think you get up first and then feel better later, or do you think you feel better first, then get up?

As you can see from these examples, the important point of this approach is not the options themselves but the impression that person addressed has a choice. Making small choices makes it easier to do certain things; like eating vegetables, taking a bath, doing homework, keeping an appointment with the worker, or even making some important changes in life.

The following 3 interventions are helpful when used with "complainant" and "customer" type clients.

5. REFRAMING - Old Wine in a New Bottle

Reframing is a technique that is accepted as helpful and useful and is used extensively in family therapy practice. It is a gentle, yet, potent way to help clients to see their predicament in a different light. This paves the way for them to find a different way to conceptualise the problem and helps to increase the possibility of finding a new solution to old problems.

Reframing is simply, an alternative, usually a positive, interpretation of troublesome behaviour which thus gives a positive meaning to the client's interaction with those in her environment. Therefore, it suggests a new and different way of behaving, freeing the client to alter behaviour and making it possible to bring about changes, while "saving face". As a result, the client sees her situation differently, and even finds solutions in a way that she did not expect.

You already have seen some examples of reframing in this manual, for example, anger can be labelled intense caring, fighting can be a sign of one's independence or a deep caring.

Examples of Reframing:

Lazy .... laid back, mellow, relaxed, taking it easy

Pushy .... assertive, in a hurry, action oriented

Impatient .... action oriented, has a high standard

Uncaring .... detached, allows room for others

Depressed .... overwhelmed, quiet, slowing down

Aggressive .... forceful, unaware of his own strength

Nagging .... shows concern, trying to bring out the best

Withdrawn .... deep thinker, thoughtful, shy, quiet

Imagine yourself thinking about someone as "depressed". The way you behave towards someone who is "depressed" is quite different from the way you behave towards someone who is "overwhelmed, quiet, or slowed down". Helping the client "reframe" her own behaviour will increase the possibility that she will think, feel, and act differently.

STEPS TOWARDS REFRAMING

1. Think about what your current interpretation is of a client's troublesome behaviour.
2. Train yourself to think of a number of alternative interpretations of the same behaviour.
3. Pick the one interpretation that seems most plausible and most fits the client's way of acting and thinking.
4. Formulate a sentence in your mind that describes a new positive interpretation.
5. Give the client the feedback on what your thoughts are.
6. The client's reaction will let you know whether your reframing fits her or not by the way she reacts. A good fit will bring a visible change in the client. Sometimes, they look stunned, shocked, amused, start to laugh, or have the "a-ha" look in their faces. When you see any of these, you have found a good fit.

Case example

Peggy, 32 years old, is a single parent of two daughters, Lisa, 14 and Melody, 11. She was referred to FBS by the intake worker following his investigation of an alleged physical and psychological abuse of 14-year-old Lisa. Lisa reports that her mother kicks her, threatens to kill her, calls her "a slut, a whore" and so on. Lisa has been in therapy herself for about 6 months, and her mother claims that therapy made her "more uppity" and pulled her out of treatment.

Grandmother reports that Peggy is angry at the whole world, and has alienated everyone in the family, and at times, even grandmother is afraid of her.

It was easy to see why everyone labels Peggy as angry, aggressive, and intimidating. She certainly came across that way to the worker. Peggy was clearly frustrated with Lisa's shoplifting, truancy, and interest in boys. When asked about what kind of trouble Lisa gives her, Peggy went into long tirades about Lisa.

Recognising the importance of building a trusting relationship with Peggy if Lisa was going to be helped, the worker started by asking whether Peggy has always been so caring about Lisa. This was enough to bring tears in her eyes, and she started to relate her special feelings for Lisa and thought that maybe she had spoiled Lisa by giving her everything she wanted, even when she had to go without things herself. Besides, Peggy desperately wanted to protect Lisa from making the same mistake she made as a teenager.

In later contacts, the worker reframed Peggy's tendency to jump into an argument with her family as her way of standing up for herself and doing what she believes is right, even when she pays a high price for it.

Parents' unreasonable expectations of children can be reframed as having high standards for them. A client's tendency to be "secretive" can be seen as her need for privacy and therefore, she should take all the time she needs to be sure that she feels safe enough to trust someone like the "welfare worker".

Case example

Ron and Betty were married when they were 18 and 17, when Betty became pregnant. Life has not been easy for them; at times Ron held two jobs to keep things going when their 3 children were younger, and now they both have to work. During one of their intense arguments about Betty's tendency to be messy and Ron's frustration with it, Betty blurted out that Ron always had "common sense" when it came to decisions about the children and that both agreed that Betty lacked in that area.

The worker immediately picked up on this and commented: "It may be true. But you certainly had enough sense to marry someone with common sense. What does that say about you?"

This little reframe changed the tone of the session from one of mutual blaming and criticism to one where they started to talk about how well they have done, given the difficult beginning they had.

6. KEEPING TRACK OF WHAT GOES WELL

"Between now and next time we see you, keep track of what goes well in your life (with your son, with your temper, with your husband, etc. or whatever would be the reverse of the client's problem) that you want to see happen again and again."

As you can see from the directive, the attention is shifted to something someone is doing well, instead of problems and failures. This task helps the client focus on what measures she takes to improve things, to notice the patterns of action and reaction in interpersonal relationships that are going well. This can give the client a feeling that she can successfully manage her life, so that she gains a sense of control.

Remember to phrase the task as when, not if. It implies that the client will overcome her urge to do undesirable things. Her attention is directed toward the positive things she does, and not the times when things go badly.

7. EXTERNALISING THE PROBLEM - Devil Made Me Do It

This technique works well with children of all ages, and some adults. It is borrowed from the works of Michael White of Australia, who started to use this approach to treat "temper" problems of children and adolescents. The strategy is to join forces with client to "fight the devil" that makes her do things that get her into trouble.

This is a good strategy to use when it is pragmatic and realistic not to fight with the client but to go along with her tendency to put the blame on external things. Therefore, the client can come up with various "monster taming" or "devil fighting" exercises to combat and to win, beating the monster or the devil that gets the client into trouble.

Some alcohol or drug abuse treatment programs basically use the same principle when it teaches abusers that the disease of the addiction takes over and controls the person. Therefore, taking the 12 steps or membership in AA is a strategy to fight the addiction by joining forces with others.

Clients, whether adolescents, adults or children, can become enthusiastic about such things as building stamina; outsmarting the sneaky, devious, and cunning temptations of alcohol; bad moods; laziness; hot temper; temptation to "flash" and other undesirable urges.

8. WORKER-TEAM (OR WORKER-SUPERVISOR) SPLIT

This is a useful intervention when the client pays a heavy psychological toll and seems unable to decide between two equally compelling options or choices, for instance, choosing to take a chance on what the future holds for her as against deciding to put up with an unhappy, at times painful, but known and familiar relationship.

When the choice seems clear and obvious to the worker, it is easy and tempting to get pulled into giving advice on what to do, only to be disappointed at the client's failure to follow through. A worker-team split is a good technique to get you out of this dilemma.

This simple technique is designed to highlight the client's ambivalence by having the worker take one side, while the team (or the invisible supervisor or a team member) takes the opposite side of the ambivalence. This way, the worker emphasises the difficulty of making the right decision while none the less framing the dilemma clearly and subtly weighing the options.

For example:

A client is at a critical point of having her children taken away. In spite of her cocaine use, she has maintained a marginal level of parenting even though she slips now and then to a potentially dangerous point. Even though she gives lip service to wanting to keep the family together, she seems to be on the fence about how willing she is to work hard to keep the family together.

A young mother was told that her 12-year-old daughter was sexually molested by her boyfriend. Medical examination and interviews with the 12-year-old were inconclusive. The client wants to be fair to her boyfriend and wants to believe her daughter but doing both is difficult. Knowing what the consequences may be, she feels extremely ambivalent and confused about what to do. She doesn't know whether she should leave the abusive relationship or stay. She can see the cost and benefit, and consequences of both choices.

HOW DOES THE WORKER-TEAM SPLIT WORK?

The primary worker always takes the positive, healthy, motivated side that is willing to take risks in the search for solution, while the team takes the other side of the ambivalence, emphasising the wish to keep things from changing.

At times the primary worker can take a "confused" stance, while the team can split into two: "one half of the team thinks you should kick your boyfriend out, while the other half the teams thinks you should keep him around, just in case he changes. I am not sure what is best for you since I can see that both sides have good points and bad points."

Case example: On the Way to the Hospital

Twenty-two-year-old Kathy makes excuses for her abusive boyfriend. While on one hand she feels angry and humiliated by the physical abuse, on the other hand she makes excuses for his violence and for his alcohol and drug abuse. Her reasoning is that when he is not under the influence, he is a most loving, thoughtful, and a helpless "little boy" who needs her badly. She has been "in love" with him since she was 17 and his family has rejected him. Besides, she has "no place to go with two children". Ken says he is humiliated by being thrown out of the apartment by the police, by her nagging, checking him up on him everywhere he goes with his friends, throwing things at him, etc.

The situation of "Kathy" exasperates FBS workers everywhere. Frequently the police and the district attorney's office become angry with such clients. Family members, friends, almost everyone becomes angry with her because when things go wrong she is frantic to enlist their help and advice, but she never follows through. Child care is neglected, the police are called, the boyfriend is evicted; they break up; everyone breathes a sigh of relief, only to see them reconcile with promises to do better when in fact, nothing has changed. Everyone is cautious, wondering when it is going to start all over again. Most FBS workers are familiar with such cases.

Following one of those stormy fights, the team became very concerned and gave her the following message during one of the sessions:

"Kathy, it is clear to all of us that you and Kenny want to do what is good for all of you and that you both are having a difficult time doing it. The team is particularly concerned about the increasing violence between you and Kenny and are very worried about both of your abilities to protect yourselves from harming each other and harming your children. The team wants you to give some serious thought to when you would say "enough is enough": on your way to a hospital with a broken neck; when one of you injures your children seriously; or on the way to the city morgue. On the other hand, I really don't know what to think about that since I know how much you want to do what is best for your children."

Kathy was visibly shaken by this, promised that she will not let the children be hurt, said she did not want to die, nor did she want to kill Kenny. Kathy eventually left the relationship following another fight.

WHAT TO DO IF YOU DO NOT WORK WITH A TEAM

Workers without a team can still make use of this approach. The simplest way is to say to the client: "Half of me thinks this way (and insert the suggestion), and the other half of me thinks that way (place another suggestion here), and frankly I am not sure which of the two is the better choice."

Another way to use the split to highlight the client's ambivalence is to say: "My many years of experience with your kind of problems would suggest you should go this way (specify one option), however, your problem is very unique and very different from most. Therefore, knowing your situation I might suggest that (the worker here suggests another option). So, I am not really sure what to suggest. I want you to think about all this and when we meet next time, tell me what steps you have taken.

The following 6 interventions are useful for "customer" type clients only.

9. KEEPING TRACK OF WHAT YOU DO WHEN YOU OVERCOME THE URGE

This intervention implies that good and positive things will happen in the client's life between sessions and the client is to watch for those positive things. This helps the client focus on what she does that helps her, and who does what to make things better.

For example, 8-year-old Naco and 10-year-old Nicolas were recently moved from a foster home to live with their grandmother when it was discovered that Naco was sexually abused in the foster home. Having lived alone for some time and now working at two jobs, grandmother was at first reluctant to take the children but agreed as their mother was in no situation to care for them because of her drug abuse.

The grandmother was quite defensive about her own child rearing practices and insisted that the mother was a good-hearted person who got sidetracked by the drug use and the influence of bad people.

Deciding to accept her world view, for the time being at least, the workers initially gave the grandmother this task: "keep track of what you notice happening with Naco and Nicolas that tells you that their living with you is good for them". Later on, the same task was phrased in more active terms:"We want you to keep track of what you do to help the children heal from the abuse".

If you have a client who sees herself as not having control of her life, this is a good way to get started. You may want to change the sentence structure gradually. Sometimes, these subtle changes are better, making it easier for the client to take credit for the improvement she will be making.

10. CHANGING A SMALL ELEMENT IN FAMILIAR PATTERNS

This is the easiest and simplest task to give to the family. All patterns and sequences around problems and solutions are rule governed and sometimes changing a small element of a pattern can make a big difference to the repetitive "same old problem".

For example, if the couple's fighting causes a problem for them, find out the details of the fighting pattern: where, how long, when, what about, who says what, what happens next, etc. Find out what is the smallest step they can change in the sequence and have them experiment with Making sure that they change the location of where they fight can make a big difference. They may agree to fight only in the bedroom, only about one topic at a time, never during a meal, or only while they are walking in the shopping mall (where there is the built-in safety of being in a public place).

A parent who is frustrated with her teenage son not getting up for school on time, for example, tends to say the same thing; the same pleading, the same lecture, the same bargaining, the same threats, and the same punishments. When workers talk to these children, they find that these children can repeat word for word what their parents say to them. Children do listen to their parents but do not follow their direction. Not knowing this, most parents tend to repeat what they say "until blue in the face" and then they become frustrated because the child does not "listen".

A mother with this problem has a number of options, all related to her no longer doing "more of the same" and doing something different. She can stop reminding him about getting up for school; she can make him "work" at home. Since he refuses to "work" at school, he should "work" at home, doing things such as washing walls, but he should not stay home and watch TV. He can be made to stay in bed all day, and not allowed to get up, so he has no TV, no music, and no entertainment whatever; his telephone can be "turned off" accidentally; there is nothing to eat and no money; and there are numerous other things that can make it more uncomfortable and inconvenient to be home rather than at school.

A couple whose fighting tends to get out of hand whenever they discuss touchy issues, can make an arrangement with each other to discuss these only in public places, such as a coffee shop, at McDonald's over a cup of coffee, or over a sandwich at a restaurant. This builds in protection against things getting out of hand. With clients who have work or job experience, the worker can suggest that every couple needs a business or staff meeting now and then and they should come to the meeting with a list of things to discuss.

With some couples, the worker can structure their "business" meetings by suggesting that the first meeting is only to list problems, the second meeting is to combine the two lists, and third meeting is to figure out what the solutions might be. This kind of step-by-step suggestion must be sufficiently different from what they did before. Such differences, however small, increase the chances of success.

Case example

Joe and Betty admitted that their disagreements on their parenting styles frequently get out of hand, and at times both of their tempers flare up and they end up hitting each other, especially if they both are under the influence of alcohol. They both agreed that it is not only bad for their marriage but is also having a serious impact on their 2 children who are beginning to mimic them by throwing things, calling each other bad names, and so on.

They report that they have never been able to work together as a team. Betty, coming from a large family in which she raised many of her younger siblings, saw herself as an expert on child care, while Joe, feeling less sure of himself as a parenting figure, was nevertheless eager to learn. Besides, he had some strong feelings about how a boy should be raised and wanted a strong input into raising his boys.

The couple were told to have two meetings between sessions. They were to go to a public place, such as, McDonald's or an inexpensive coffee shop for these meetings. The goal for the first meeting was only to air their ideas on parenting, without trying to convince each other, or trying to solve the differences. Each could pretend to listen if they disagreed with the other's views but not to express their own view. If they finished expressing their views, they were free to do anything that they both wished, such as, go to a movie, go for a drive, or whatever they agreed would be enjoyable.

During the second meeting which was to occur within 48 hours of the first meeting, each was to offer their views of what the compromise would look like and what the action plan would be that was needed to implement the compromised view. Again, they were to only air the opinions, and not to attempt to implement any of their ideas.

Discussion:

It is easy to see that when clients are offered and follow step-by-step instructions that are tailored to their unique needs and situations, their safety is assured and they are likely to develop some solution finding skills.

11. SECRET SIGN

Credit for this intervention goes to a gifted group of therapists in Denver (Charlie Johnson and Yvonne Dolan) who told me about its effectiveness with violence-prone families. This works well even when small children are involved.

Since safety is the most important factor when working with families where violence has been a problem, this is worth a try. As a part of an understanding or a contract, the worker and all family members have an agreement on a specific object (such as a doll, a family treasure, a special toy, a souvenir item, or an ugly gift from Aunt Harriet, etc.) that everyone will use as a signal. Whenever anyone in the family is afraid of violence, inappropriate touching, or a threat of violence has been made by any family member, anyone in the family is free to take the item. The disappearance of the item is a signal to the rest of the family that someone is scared and therefore someone must call the worker or the police.

This kind of safety measure gives everyone in the family a sense of control; it is something everybody can do to protect themselves and the family.

12. SECRET COMFORTING NOTE

This is another idea borrowed from my colleague in Denver (Yvonne Dolan) that is helpful with an extremely damaged, or traumatised client or someone in a crisis. This intervention relies on and takes advantage of a person's innate self-healing capacity.

Have the client think of a word or a symbol of comforting thoughts or a sentence that has a special meaning, such as, a grandmother who was particularly nurturing but who is dead now; a soothing and relaxing picture in one's mind; a phrase that has a special positive meaning to the client. Have the client write that word or phrase in her non-dominant hand, and have her carry that special piece of paper with her wherever she goes. (When the client uses the non-dominant hand to write with there is extra effort required and the words may appear to be written in a childlike way). Whenever she becomes scared, insecure, or frightened, she can take it out and be comforted. When the note is worn out or the meaning changes, the client can make another note.

13. PRETENDING THAT THE MIRACLE HAS HAPPENED

When you get a good description of a miracle, pictured in a concrete, realistic, and measurable manner (see Chapter 7 for details on Miracle Questions), have the client pick a day that will be convenient for her, and on that day she is told "pretend that the miracle has happened and do everything you would do when the miracle happens, and keep track of what you notice that is different about yourself, about your family, and how other people react to you."

Case example: Fooling Parents with Miracle

15-year-old Rex was a pro at "therapy", having been through in-patient treatment several times and outpatient treatment (individual, group, and family counselling), he not only abused alcohol and drugs but also was a minor drug dealer. He was squeaking through school, with frequent truancy, and failing grades even though he was very intelligent. His parents were constantly angry at him, feeling worn out, and were considering a Child In Need of Protective Service (CHIPS) petition as the final solution to their frustration.

When asked the miracle question during the assessment phase, Rex detailed all the things he would do when he had a miracle: "I will get up at 6 o'clock on my own, eat a good breakfast, get to the bus on time, get to school, stay in school, pay attention, come home, do homework, talk with the family about the day during dinner, help clean up, do homework, maybe talk to friends on the phone, and go to bed."

The team decided to take advantage of his tendency to be secretive, sneaky, and so on, and thus gave him the following intervention.

Rex was to "pretend that the miracle happened one day of his choice each week during the next two weeks" and do all the things he would do when the miracle happened. He should keep secret from his parents which day his "miracle day" was a secret from his parents, but pay attention to whether his parents noticed anything different about those days. The parents were to guess which day they thought that Rex was having his "miracle day" and to let him know which day they thought it was, not by discussing it but by giving him a small reward, such as a pat on the back, cooking his favourite food, or taking him out for an ice cream, etc.

Of course the parents were wrong in guessing which days they thought were "the miracle days"; they ended up with 6 days of miracles instead of the expected 2.

The next step is for the client to repeat the "miracle days" as often as she can.

14. PINK ELEPHANT

This has been used successfully with children of all ages and in all cultural settings. An adapted version of this intervention has been used with adults, also.

It is an ideal intervention for someone who feels helpless, powerless or victimised in social relationships. Some children who are picked out as a target of "bullying" or "teasing" repeatedly respond in a predictable manner; that is they cower, look scared, or avoid eye contact with the other children who tease or bully them. As soon as the "bullies" approach them, the child usually runs away, bursts into tears, or tattles to the teachers, or other adults. Such a reaction, in turn, of course brings on more teasing and bullying.

Workers can give these children a "secret weapon". When they appear ready to be a "customer", give the child this directive:

Case example 1

"Jason, I want you to keep this a top secret. You cannot tell anyone about this and this has to be kept an absolute secret for it to work. Whenever Jerry and his friends come near you and you think they are going to start teasing you I want you to do 3 things. First, you imagine a huge pink elephant ("Have you seen a pink elephant?" "No? Well, he only comes out in secret") dropping from the sky and about to land on Jerry's head and squish him flat. Of course you can see it but Jerry cannot see it. Second, every time you see him I want you to imagine that he lost all his hair and all his teeth. So he is bald headed and toothless. Third, I want you to imagine that his fly is open. Got it? When I see you next time I want you to tell me how things are different for you."

Case example 2: A Naked Boss

A woman was in tears as she described her encounters with her boss whom she described as "ranting and raving at me". She liked her job very much, saw a potential for moving up but she was on the verge of quitting because of the intense conflict with her boss. The pattern she described was similar to Jason's; she would burst into tears, get upset, and thus become less productive, which in turn invited her boss's wrath.

Since the pattern was similar, it was decided to suggest to her the modified version of the "pink elephant". It was suggested to the woman that next time she has a run-in with her boss, she should pretend that her boss is stark naked when he yells and screams at her.

She reported at the following session that she had discovered that her boss did that to everyone in the office, that it was not her problem but that he had poor interpersonal skills, and she decided not to take it personally. She decided to stay on the job.

Discussion:

Children like Jason, who feel victimised and powerless, need some secret weapon that will give them a sense of power and ability to control their life. When Jason imagines revenge on the other child who picks on him, he is likely to smile, and act more confident, not likely to cower or run away. Something is different about Jason. This interrupts their typical interaction patterns. The same principle worked with the young woman and her boss.

15. PREDICTION TASK

At times clients report that exceptions to the problem do happen sometimes but see them as not being within their control. They describe these exceptions as if they happen completely randomly and occur spontaneously. Since they cannot describe exactly how these exceptions occur, it is not reasonable to tell them to repeat these exceptions. The following task helps clients to realise that those exceptions may be much more within their control than they thought.

A client is told to "make a prediction" at the end of each day as to whether she will have a "good day" or "bad day" the following day. The next day, she is to go about her usual routine. At the end of the day, she is to review the day and record whether it was indeed a "good day" or "bad day" and make another prediction for the following day. She is to repeat this until the next appointment.

Keeping a careful comparison of what the client predicted and how the day actually turned out will produce some interesting insights into the client's ability to make what appears to be a random or spontaneous exception into a deliberate one. My experience is that most clients predict many more "bad days" than they actually have. In the process of reviewing each day with the worker, the client discovers that her week turned out to be much better than she thought. Clients will also discover many more deliberate exceptions than they thought they had.

The worker can encourage and enhance the client's discovery of ways to "do more of" such deliberate exceptions, thus, expanding her successes.

Case example

11-year-old Marcus was brought to the attention of the worker because of his long-standing problem of bed-wetting. His foster mother was frustrated with the hassle and had tried everything she could to be helpful, which caused her even more frustration.

In talking with Marcus alone, it was reasonably clear that he was pretty embarrassed about the bed-wetting and wanted to solve the problem. Various questions indicated that he was ready to be a "customer". He would like to go to summer camp like other boys, sleep over at a friend's house, and so on, but he was reluctant to do so because of his problem.

Close questioning revealed that Marcus had many exceptions, such as, when he slept over with his cousin at his grandma's house, and at least once or twice a week even when he slept at home in his own bed. Since he was unable to explain what the difference was between those nights he had a dry bed or when he had a wet bed, he saw these exceptions as random and completely out of his control. The team decided the prediction task would be appropriate.

He was given a daily chart where he could make a prediction just before going to bed of whether or not he would have a dry bed. The following morning he was to record whether his prediction was correct or not. If his prediction was proved wrong, he was to account for the incorrect prediction. If a correct prediction was made, he was to explain how he knew that. Either way he could be complimented for knowing what behaviour was linked to his bed-wetting.

In the meantime, the foster mother was told that Marcus was old enough to take care of changing the sheets, laundering them when necessary, and she was instructed to completely stay out of checking his bed in the morning, reprimanding or scolding him about any wet beds. She was also to make a prediction of whether she thought Marcus would have a dry or wet bed each night and keep track of the outcome. Both Marcus and the foster mother were to keep their predictions secret from each other and not to discuss them.

The following week Marcus proudly produced his record of his experiment. He had many more nights when his bed was dry. He explained that he had cut down on drinking liquid and told himself he was going to have a dry bed. He added that perhaps he was doing better in school also and got along much better with his foster mother.

There are more complicated intervention techniques that can be borrowed from the family therapy field. But these 15 interventions listed are easy to follow, simple to do, and most clients of DSS respond well. As you can see already, these intervention tasks are designed to elicit exceptions and to interrupt the patterns around problematic behaviours. The result is that they empower clients to discover and use their own resources. Along with good interviewing skills described in Chapter 6 the techniques described here will be quite sufficient to get started to "do something different" with the majority of FBS cases.

Ten
SPECIAL PROBLEMS

This chapter describes some practical strategies and techniques that workers can use in their daily encounters and which will leave clients with feelings of hope and of some success This chapter is not designed to be a comprehensive coverage of the various problem topics. Workers are encouraged to study other more comprehensive works which deal with the treatment issues of each topic individually.

LOOKING AT THE WHOLE FAMILY
It is easy to categorise a family as a "violence case", "incest case", "abuse case", or "drug abuse case" and so on. This is a dangerous practice because workers tend to concentrate on "the problem" and forget the people behind it. There is no single, typical picture of a violent family, incest family, or a drug or alcohol abuser. There are so many variations in family and problem configurations that such categorisation is almost useless in directing what the worker should do.

It is not helpful to "rush in" with a treatment plan to impose on the family. Individualised treatment, that is, a treatment that makes sense to the client, seems reasonable from her world view, and is congruent with the way she does things, will reduce worker frustration. Keep in mind that all families are different and, therefore, two families with the same drug abuse problem may require very different treatments.

A. MANAGEMENT OF CRISIS
Poor, "marginally functioning", ethnic minority, or multi-problem families are thought to "thrive on crisis" and to "live from crisis to crisis", or it is believed that "crisis gives them some excitement in their dull lives". I believe such misconceptions about these families come from the fact that the client contacts with the Social Service Department are typically sporadic and center around crises. Furthermore, workers tend to ignore these families' successful management of their lives between crises, noticing only the problems that trigger the crises.

WHAT IS A CRISIS?
A crisis can mean that something new is happening or that something different needs to happen but is not happening. Crisis signals a danger and an opportunity, that is, a crisis can be a signal that a problem could become worse if some change is not made, and it can also be an opportunity to bring about the needed changes in a family unit. Therefore the worker's goal need not be limited to restoring the status quo but it can also be to improve the functioning of the family unit.

So, what can the FBS worker do to help turn the crisis into an opportunity? The most common reaction to a crisis is to overreact by taking drastic measures. It is important that the worker stays "cool headed" and analyses the situation before taking such steps. Slowing down in the middle of a crisis is not easy to do but it does help.

The following are some guidelines for turning the crisis into an opportunity for growth:

1. Find out what is different this time.

Why is the fight worse this time? (Clearly they fought many times before, so what is different about this fight?) Why is the client more upset this time about the loss of a job, the school calling, the child spilling the milk, the husband leaving, so that events touch off a crisis this time?

Usually, what is different this time is not measured by the seriousness or the gravity of the "problem" itself but the meaning or interpretation of the event for the person involved. They have been through the same thing many times before but somehow it means something different this time. Find out what that different meaning is to the client.

2. What is the combination of event and reaction?

The trigger is hard to determine: what is the external reality that makes a crisis and what is the internal reaction to these factors?

Case example

With great determination, Brenda finally finished a job training program and found a job that she thought had potential for promotion with increased income and job security. She still believed this job held the promise of a career. However, during her probationary period on the job she received many warnings about the phone calls from school about Jimmy's behaviour problems. In spite of the fact that they had many conversations during which she warned Jimmy about the danger of the loss of her job and what it meant to the family's future, nothing seemed to help.

She came close to losing her job one more time because of the latest phone call from the school, which Brenda described as "the straw that broke the camel's back". Exasperated with Jimmy's lack of cooperation, frustrated with having to battle with her ex-husband over the visitation of the children and her boss's insensitivity to her single-parent status, Brenda admitted that she "went after Jimmy with a baseball bat" in spite of her determination to get off welfare.

The worker spent a great deal of time with Brenda talking about what was different about this one last phone call that got her to react as she did, and how she could have handled the stress differently. Given Jimmy's tendency to be outspoken with teachers, his "class clown" behaviours, and not taking his studies seriously, Brenda agreed that she was likely to get another phone call from the school. She decided on steps that she could take next time not to jeopardise her job and "go off the handle".

3. How did the client handle past crises successfully?

It is always helpful for the worker to find out how the client successfully handled past crises similar to the current one. If the client has survived even worse crises than the current one, the worker needs to know what she did then and what aspects of her action can be applied here. Such transference is helpful to the client and conveys to her that we all learn from our successes and mistakes.

4. "How come things are not worse?"

As you find out the details of the crisis, pay attention to what the client did right to contain the crisis so that it did not get worse.

Case example

15-year-old Tara overdosed on her mother's tranquilizers and had passed out on the living room floor when her mother returned from the laundromat. This was the first such episode. At first the mother thought Tara was catching up with her sleep, at worst, maybe experimenting with drugs, and left her to sleep. Tara managed to signal to her mother that she needed to go to hospital, and her mother responded promptly.

Later when things calmed down, the worker spent a considerable amount of time helping both Tara and mother figure out how they both had done many things right in the crisis: how Tara figured out that she needed to signal to her mother that she needed help ,and how her mother had enough sense to listen to·Tara's attempt at communication. Tara's initiatives were praised, credit was given to Tara for having enough trust in her mother to let her know immediately. Credit was also given to the mother for responding to that trust and getting the medical attention Tara needed.

Obviously, the reason for Tara's "cry for help" needed to be addressed, but the early intervention in giving clients credit builds a positive relationship for later work. Later, Tara was able to discuss with the worker the intense peer pressure and the fights she had in school, the threats of violence she received, the fear of "being jumped on", the troubles with teachers, and so on.

5. "What have you learned about yourself (or your family) from this crisis?"

After the crisis is over, it is always useful for the worker to help the client review the whole event. Each crisis can be viewed as having taught all of us something new about ourselves. Thus, asking the following questions would not only be role modelling but would also help the client to "save face".

"In looking back over the last couple of weeks, what do you suppose you learned about yourself that you did not know?"

"Is that new for you? Did it surprise you?"

"What would you say you did differently this time?"

"What do you suppose your mother (or other significant person in the client's life) would say you learned from having gone through what you have just been through?"

6. Not all crises are the same.

Remember that what is a crisis for one family is not necessarily the same crisis for another, even if the incidents are identical. Each client's definition of crisis is very different and their experience is very different. Accept the client's definition as valid and relevant to her. Except around issues such as child protection, workers should not impose their values on the client.

Case example

The author was once involved in a study of survival factors of breast cancer patients. A segment of the study was to interview patients on how they managed other crises in their lives, in order to develop a list or repertoire of skills that patients can use. One 48-year-old lady reported that the most traumatic crisis she had ever experienced in her life was when she was 22 years old. What could possibly be more traumatic than a diagnosis of cancer? It was when her fiancée jilted her, broke off the engagement and married some other girl. Even though the lady knew that it would have been a disastrous marriage had she gone through with it, she explained that it was the most devastating experience she had ever had even worse than the news that she had breast cancer in her mid-40's.

The lesson of this case is that not all crises are the same for everyone, but that individually they can be very different.

7. What is the first, early signal that a crisis is brewing?

Most clients can describe the early signs, "vibes", "hunches" or some clues that "something is not going right". Workers need to spend some time discussing these early signs with families in detail. Questions to ask are:
a) What is the first clue to you that this argument is likely to become fighting?
b) What are the steps you can take to stop the argument getting out of hand? What worked in the past that might work again and what new steps can you think of taking?
c) How come other similar situations did not lead to crises; who did what, how, and when differently, so that you handled it? What have you learned from this?
d) What are the conditions or triggers that are likely to lead to a crisis? Are you more likely to fight when: you are tired; have been drinking; when the money runs out; have been under more stress?
e) What are the earliest signs that "something is going to go wrong"?
f) When you have discussed these questions, how can you help the family figure out what steps they need to take?
g) After a crisis, discuss it with the family and find out what they learned from it. Such "debriefing" helps the family to learn to do the same for themselves.

Case example

This was the first marriage for Terry and second for Gary; both agreed that it had been a "nightmare" since the wedding. Each had had considerable difficulties in previous relationships. Terry was raped at 19, hospitalised after she went "psychotic" following the rape and was on "anti-psychotic" medication; she had joined a "fundamental church", then had fallen out of it; she could only handle the third-shift job in a nursing home. Many attempts at relationships did not work out for her.

Gary's ex-wife left him for another man; some years ago he cut off ties with his adoptive mother entirely; he had been recovering from alcohol abuse but still "messed" with drugs now and then; he had been a "self-help group junkie" for several years; he flew into a rage whenever he "saw" Terry "primping herself" in public; he was "leaving the marriage" one day, then was in love with Terry, the next.

Since the wedding the couple had had a series of crises, resulting in non-stop arguing which usually ended only when both were exhausted or hungry, and once ended in physical violence. Every holiday, forgotten birthday, phone call from Terry's mother, picture of a previous relationship, and everything and anything, could trigger the chain- reaction pattern: one accused, the other defended and counter-accused, past grievances were listed, there were threats of leaving, and it would end in making up, only for the cycle to be repeated almost every week. Gary was once taken to a hospital for an "anxiety attack" and Terry described herself as going "psychotic" during one of these fights.

A useful treatment strategy with this couple was to review and anticipate potential crises and debrief the past crisis during each contact. Each session was spent thoroughly going over each item as listed below :

a) There was a review of who did what, and how, to diffuse the upset so that each episode did not end in violence.

b) Compliments were given to whichever of them had taken steps to not overreact.

c) There was an examination of forthcoming events that might trigger either one to get upset.

d) Since any review of the past events only triggered the blaming, accusing, defending, counter-blaming pattern, the worker focused on successful strategies to avert future crises.

During one of the sessions, Terry blurted out that she would get really upset if Gary forgot about Valentine's day. It turned out that Gary had disappointed her during Christmas, Thanksgiving, birthday, many week-ends, and that this usually ended in big arguments. A large portion of the session was spent reviewing past arguments and previewing of what she might do differently next time so that there was a chance of ending in a different way. Terry decided to lower her expectations of Gary about such things. This was reframed as her way of learning to accept him because she loved him.

B. MULTI-PROBLEM FAMILIES

At times, some cases have so many problems and issues that even a seasoned worker can get overwhelmed and feel lost as to where to begin. Many multi-problem cases can have one or more of the following components: chronic unemployment, frequent job changes, chronic physical and mental illness, marital conflict, truancy, delinquent behaviour of one or more children, poor academic performance, long-standing inter-generational conflicts for example between mother and grandmother, series of unstable relationships in a mother's life, over-involved extended families of origin, chronic mental illness, drug and alcohol abuse, continued drug and alcohol use during pregnancy, sexual abuse of children by the mother's boyfriend, mother's inability to protect the children, and so on.

Sometimes doing less accomplishes more and going slow gets there faster. The common and immediate reaction to multi-problem families is to become overwhelmed, to "bring out the cavalry", and to parcel out the problems and treatment plans accordingly.

For example, each child is sent to separate therapists, in-patient drug treatment, or family therapy. Someone is put on medication, day care for the children and job training are arranged. The family is bombarded with various programs, out of a belief that "more and quicker is better". Not only is such a massive infusion of services confusing to the client, but also, clients cannot realistically manage all those schedules and appointments. With such a massive overdose of services it is difficult to know what makes a difference. In addition, such an approach has the effect of fragmenting the family. The clients are often given conflicting suggestions and demanding schedules of appointments with professionals. Some treatment programs conflict with each other and some treatment plans are made by treatment providers without consulting the families or the other service providers. The result is unrealistic, unmanageable plans that the families cannot follow through. This frequently results in the family being labelled as "unmotivated", "unreachable" and so on.

Since you are working with any number of combinations of problems listed here, it is easy to move in and take over the solution finding process. Remember the message that has been consistent throughout this book: the more clients solve their own problems, the more empowering it is to them. The following are some guidelines you need to keep in mind as you proceed.

1. Do not panic; be calm and follow these steps.
2. Ask the client what is the most urgent problem that she needs to solve first. Follow her direction, not yours. Be sure the goal is small, realistically achievable, and simple.
3. Ask yourself who is most bothered by the problem? Make sure it is not you; you do not want to be "the customer" for your own services.
4. Get a good picture of how her life would change when that one goal is achieved. Find out how her life would be different. (See Chapter 5 for setting goals.)

5. Stay focused on solving that one problem first. Do not let the fact that the client is overwhelmed affect you. Stay focused with the first goal until it is achieved.
6. Find out in detail how the client has made things better in the past. She needs to know what her own successful strategies are, which she can then apply to other problems.
7. Be sure to compliment the client on even the smallest progress and achievements. Always give clients the credit.
8. When one problem is solved, then review with the client how she solved it. What did she do that worked? How did she figure out doing it that way? In a new context of success, what does she need to do to solve the second problem? Remember that this is also a chance to empower her.

C. VIOLENCE IN THE FAMILY

Psychological or physical violence in the family, whether between adults or from adult to child, is the most distressing kind of case that workers encounter in their work. In spite of the many legal measures that exist in our community to handle such problems, it is always extremely stressful for workers to encounter any form of violence. It reminds us of human frailty and our own vulnerability, and at times it becomes difficult to maintain hope for the client. Workers must be particularly alert to their personal issues regarding violence.

NOT ALL VIOLENCE IS THE SAME

Yet, not all violence cases are the same. There is a rough pattern, and recent research information sheds new light on the causes and treatment of violence, but in the absence of definitive research data that points to a comprehensive treatment program it is difficult to come up with one. What seems to be true, however, is that some programs, such as groups like Parents Anonymous, self-help groups, education about the cycles of violence, are very helpful and useful. But not all clients are able to make use of these groups or existing programs. Therefore, it is necessary to individualise the treatment to fit the unique circumstances of the individual.

Management of violence is a very confusing issue because our society's response to the problem of violence is two-pronged. One response is to deal with it using legal means, making the punishment fit the crime; the other approach is to see it as an illness. Therefore, prevention and treatment is seen as a logical approach to cure. Whether the solution lies in social control or treatment is difficult to say, since there is no evidence that one is more successful than the other. Currently both methods are used not very successfully.

DOMESTIC VIOLENCE

Many studies indicate that strong measures; such as, calling the police, arresting the abuser, leaving the home, moving to a shelter, are all useful to a point. Since most abusers are not likely to seek help until they are forced to do so, these steps should be taken whenever warranted.

Those clients who are willing, with some encouragement, to use the existing community resources, such as the shelter, self-help groups, and other training groups, should be encouraged to do so. The majority of clients, however, are not likely to follow through on referrals to such resources. For them, the FBS worker may be the only person who can make some impact on their pattern of violence and, therefore, the role of the FBS worker becomes crucial. You may be the only person who can make a difference since you have an entry into the family system.

Each case is unique and different from any other case and has its own set of problem configurations, resources, history and patterns of violence, motivation, commitment and investment in the relationship. Therefore, how you treat one violence case may be very different from how you treat another.

The more flexible your options and your approaches, the more likely it is that you will be able to individualise your treatment strategies, and therefore, reach more clients. The more options you have in a case, the less likely you are to feel overwhelmed and stuck.

By the same token, clients also need to have many strategies and options available to them, such as either party leaving the scene, taking time out from arguments, being aware of what is the trigger point, walking out of the house, discussing emotionally charged issues only in public places (where there is a built-in safety measure), making sure that weapons are taken out of the house, both partners making sure not to "push the buttons" that trigger the emotional reactions at the wrong time, and learning to postpone the emotionally charged decisions.

Case example

43-year-old Tom was a Vietnam veteran with a long history of medical, psychiatric, and drug abuse problems. His second marriage to Steffie had been rocky and turbulent for the past 8 years, and during one of their many separations, Steffie had an affair. Recently Tom had become abusive and threatened to shoot her with his gun, at which point Steffie left for a shelter.

Being unemployed, and perhaps unemployable, because of a back injury he sustained as a construction worker, Tom had taken over the homemaker's role since Steffie went to work as a beautician. To earn extra cash, Steffie had customers coming to the house in the evenings while Tom cooked, cleaned, and took care of their 8-year-old son. While Tom's depression increased, Steffie became increasingly resentful at having to support him financially with no hope of any change in sight.

Making this transition from the "macho" world of the construction worker, burly and tough-talking Tom had been "going through hell" for the past 2 years of unemployment. His temper would flare up and he would become violent toward Steffie, especially when he felt unappreciated, nagged at, demeaned because of having to ask for money from Steffie. Both wanted to make it work "for the children's sake" (15-year-old Steffie's daughter and an 8-year-old son from this marriage.)

It was found that discussion of emotionally charged issues, such as money, sex, Steffie's long working hours, Tom's poor cooking and laundry and so on, were frequently the triggers for reactions culminating in violence. During the stay at the shelter they found that discussion of the same issues on the phone was less likely to trigger emotions. The couple came up with this discovery and decided that they would both make sure that they carried plenty of change with them at all times. Whenever they needed to discuss trigger issues they agreed to do so only on the phone.

Case example

Joe was a 29-year-old "over the road" truck driver, which means that he drove a large truck across the country. His work schedule varied, depending on where he was sent. He usually left home early Monday morning and would sometimes not return until Friday night, or sometimes he would be "on the road" for 2 - 3 weeks. He was tearful when he called the hotline one Sunday morning asking for help with his violent temper. He related that he had "sent" his wife to the hospital on a Friday night during one of those episodes when he would just "go off". When finally seen in an emergency session with the author a couple hours later, Joe was still shaken with remorse and shame. Even though his wife was invited to come to the session with Joe, she chose to sit in the car and refused to come in because she was embarrassed to show her injuries.

Joe related that he had been like a "walking time bomb" all his life. Since his early days, he got into many fights and could have easily killed someone with his violent temper. He recounted some hair-raising incidents during which he would go after several men alone and so scared them that they usually would flee. He reported that his alcohol use did not seem to make any difference in the frequency and intensity of his temper since he could be just as violent without any drinking. He confessed, however, that his violence was most frequent at home. There had been times when he was shocked to find himself choking his wife, when he had knocked her to the ground, given her many bruises, and on several occasions she had gone to hospital with broken bones. He would usually apologise profusely afterwards and promise never to do it again. This pattern was repeated almost weekly, not always ending in violence. He reported that he was critical of his wife, yelled at her, and accused her of being responsible for even minor frustrations at home.

Over the years, his wife, Sandy, was repeatedly advised by her family and friends to leave Joe. Once she finally called the shelter for battered women and made an arrangement to go there with the two boys but changed her mind at the last moment and went to look for Joe in a bar instead and brought him home. So, what was different this time since she had been to the hospital before? He hit her on the left ear so badly that her eardrum could have been damaged for life. The doctor at the hospital informed them that there was a possibility that she could have lost her hearing permanently as a result.

Curious about his close on 10 years of "over the road" truck driving without incident and his report that he had even earned "a safety award", the therapist kept asking how he managed to not lose his temper on the road. Highway driving for days and weeks, encountering all types of drivers and situations would be the most stressful situation for most people. Joe, in a matter-of-fact manner, related that he considered it to be his job. And in an equally matter-of-fact manner, related that he never drank alcohol, nor used drugs while on the road. Strongest stuff he drank was coffee, he said proudly. He added that even though he became irritated with his supervisor who made unrealistic demands on his driving schedules he never lost his temper. In fact, he proudly related that when he quit the company the year before, his boss had asked him to return, offering him a pay increase. However, whenever he got on the CB radio with Sandy, which was his way to keep in touch with his family, he would easily "blow a fuse", be critical of her and lose his temper. He thought that she deserved to be "treated as a lady" and listed many reasons for this.

Viewing this "on the road" behaviour as an exception to his problems, the therapist kept pursuing how he managed his "on the job" behaviours and to "keep his cool" with other drivers on the road for long periods. He was surprised to find himself answering "I don't dare lose my temper on the job because I could lose my job". He said he needed the job to support his family financially and that he was proud of having done it for the past 8 years of marriage. While on the job, he maintained a sense of humour, and had perfect control over his emotions and behaviours. He had never lost his temper with his two children (aged 4 and 6), and never abused them, and thought that perhaps Sandy criticised him for being too lenient with them. He thought his children were "funny", he loved to wrestle with them, play with them, and was generous with affection and love for them. Use of scaling questions indicated that he was highly motivated to "keep the family" together.

At the end of the session, after the intra-session consultation with the team, the therapist gave the following feedback to Joe.

a) He was complimented for recognising the problem and taking steps, such as calling the hotline, coming in for a session on Sunday, and for having taken a big step by admitting that he had a problem.

b) He was complimented for taking responsibility for his violence, for not blaming his wife or external events, and for recognising that she deserved to be treated as a lady.

c) He was complimented for taking his job seriously and for having learned what he needed to do to be good at it. Clearly he loved his family very much since he was a hard worker and wanted to be a good husband and a father.

d) It would not be an easy task to turn around his life-long problem of violent temper. But since he had already learned how do a good job at his work, his next task was to learn to do a better job as a family man and a husband.

e) Since he was scheduled to be "on the road" for 3 weeks before returning home, it would be a good opportunity for him to learn more about his "on the job" behaviours. Therefore, he was asked to keep track of how he was learning to do a better job as a husband while he talked to Sandy on the radio.

During a session a week later Sandy supported Joe's view. Although she had thought about leaving Joe many times, she had no real plan to leave Joe since she "loved him very much". Her most recent medical check-up had revealed that, fortunately, she would not lose her hearing. She was well-informed of her legal right to protection but insisted that she would never report Joe to the police since he was a good father and a good provider and that she really had every intention to keep the family together. She was hopeful this time since this was the first time Joe was seeking help.

Subsequent follow-up contacts revealed that Joe was doing remarkably well and there had not been a single episode of violence in the 6 months follow-up. Sandy was continually amazed at Joe's ability to "just walk away"from things which previously could have triggered him to explode.

REMINDER FOR THE WORKER

Since violence, physical, sexual, or verbal, tends to evoke strong emotional reactions towards clients, it is crucial that FBS workers seek help from peers, supervisor, and consultant, in order to maintain their neutrality and not take sides with family members.

The most difficult and yet important things to remember in treating cases where there is repeated violence are:

a) how not to side with the woman victim against the male perpetrator,

b) to refrain from forcing decisions on the woman to leave the relationship. Her family, friends, neighbours, previous workers, all gave the same advice. Since she did not follow their suggestion, you do not want to repeat it.

A better way to handle the situation is to gently repeat questions such as, "What will make you say to yourself and to your boyfriend, 'enough is enough'" or "What does your boyfriend have to do before you will say 'this is enough; I deserve better than this'".

SEXUAL ABUSE

It is estimated by the Planned Parenthood study (1985) that at least 1 in 4 girls and 1 in 8 boys are sexually molested before reaching adulthood. The perpetrator in the majority of cases is a family member or a close friend of the family. Clearly, it is a family problem and many studies document that family treatment is the most effective approach for both adult and sibling sexual abuse.

Sexual abuse of children is traumatic, devastating, humiliating and degrading to the children and can leave a profound psychological mark. Clearly the Child

Protection Service and FBS workers should be trained to provide the most updated, effective treatment approaches that maximise the healing process. Since the FBS workers enter into the family system after abuse has been discovered, the primary task is to protect the child from further abuse, and start the healing process for the child and family as soon as possible.

A combination of punishment and treatment can be effective. Treatment should be focused on empowering the child, strengthening the mother-child relationship, and putting the mother or grandparent or some other capable adult in charge of safety and protection of the child.

Since there are many complex legal and treatment issues related to the sexual abuse case it calls for specialised treatment approaches, with a view to safety, prevention, empowering the child, and preserving family ties. Before a referral to another agency is made, the following questions should be considered.

1. Is the adult in the family able to follow through the referral?
2. Will individual treatment fragment the family, which is already suffering from inappropriate generational boundaries?
3. What is the first task for the family?
4. What are the worker's criteria for safety for the child?
5. Do existing resources in the community meet the family's needs right now? Will they do so in the future?
6. What can the worker do to make sure that the "cure is not worse than the disease?"

Workers need to be familiar with the current policies on handling both adult sexual abuse cases and sibling sexual abuse cases.

WHAT TO DO WHEN THERE HAS BEEN ABUSE WHILE IN TREATMENT

The constant juggling involved in fulfiling two roles is confusing to the worker and the client alike. The roles of social control agent, and treatment provider (healing, soothing, nurturing) often seem to clash and conflict with each other. This is the most difficult aspect of FBS. Yet, the worker's role is not only to punish the client, but is also to strengthen the family relationships, thus, a further incident of abuse is less likely to occur. Gauging what is the most ethical, responsible, and legal way to behave as a professional is not a simple matter. Each case we work with calls for balancing between what is legally and ethically a responsible thing to do. For each situation, we must continually struggle to maintain this balance since there is no simple formula to rely on.

One option is for the primary worker to remain treatment oriented and be the "good" person, while the secondary worker can be the "heavy hand" that enforces the control element of the law. Ideally, both the social control and treatment stem from the same goal: to strengthen the emotional bond of the family unit, thus giving a foundation for stability and health.

When working without a team, a frank and open discussion of the worker's dilemma with the client is very helpful. Even when the worker recommends to the court the removal of a child from a home, if he does so with respect for the client's dignity, my experience is that the client will be receptive to working with him again. Most clients know right from wrong and it is better for the worker to assume that. Once again, it is important for the worker to keep in mind that each client and each case is different. All sexual abuse cases are not the same. Each case is unique and different from any other sexual abuse case, therefore, the treatment needs to be individually tailored to fit the situation.

ALCOHOL AND DRUG ABUSE

It is estimated that somewhere between 50-80% of FBS cases have drug- and alcohol-related problems. Therefore, each FBS worker must have some knowledge and skill in conducting assessments of how a client's drug and alcohol abuse is interfering with her ability to function as a parent.

There are many claims and counter-claims about the most effective, efficient, or successful treatment methods and models espoused by many experts. It is a difficult period for practitioners who must work "in the trenches" every day. While we are still waiting for conclusive data from research to tell us what might be the most appropriate treatment method for which kind of client, the available data suggests that an individualised treatment approach works the best. The exhaustive study by the Institute Of Medicine (1990) strongly advocates preventive measures and early interventions, an individualised approach, and recognition of the validity and value of non-traditional treatment.

Most experts in the field agree that the success rate is poor in alcohol treatment, approximately 10% success rate for long-term sobriety (4 years or longer). On the other hand, it is generally accepted that most treatment has the positive outcome of a reduction of alcohol consumption and an improvement in the quality of life for two-thirds of those who undergo treatment. Therefore, it poses serious questions as to whether the treatment methods are unsuccessful or should the criteria for success be revised. Many advocate (Miller, 1985, 1990) that total abstinence should not be the sole criterion for successful outcome.

FBS workers cannot ignore the cost of treatment involved because of the economic realities of the client population. Much of the outcome research data indicates that there is no appreciable difference in outcome between short-term and the traditional long term treatment of alcohol abuse (Fingerette, 1988; Hester and Miller, 1989; Holden, 1986, 1987).

Many in-patient treatment programs for drug and alcohol abuse are moving towards a shorter period of stay in treatment facilities because of the rising costs. For many clients, and especially those who participate in Health Maintenance Organisation programs, the in-patient stay becomes shorter and shorter, reducing to 14 days, 10 days, and even in-home detoxification. The traditional 28 days of treatment is no longer the rule. Most common is the 5-7 days of in-patient detoxification under medical supervision, followed by day treatment programs and outpatient treatment, self-help programs such as the Serenity Club, AA, and the sponsor system.

Most Social Service Department programs recognise the serious nature of substance abuse and its devastating effects on families. They offer a variety of services designed to minimise such effects, and thus utilise the expertise of the substance abuse counsellors. Most FBS programs have access to such services. Coordination of services and the cooperation of FBS workers and special services are crucial to success.

As most treatment programs have high relapse rates, the emphasis should be on changing the client's environment so that it is conducive to maintaining abstinence when clients return home from the program. Clients who return to the same family and social network of the abusing environment and life-style are at high risk of relapse. Many studies conclude that the success rate is higher when the abuser has family support or a meaningful job, as these give strong motivation for treatment.

Since most of the existing treatment models rely on voluntary participation, acknowledgement of problems and acceptance of treatment, the FBS worker might be the only professional person who has access to those clients who will not avail themselves of treatment programs of their own accord. Therefore, it is crucial that the workers in the FBS program have knowledge and familiarity of working with substance abuse problems so that they can make use of the opportunities that their contacts with such clients offer.

The following are some helpful suggestions for workers, which are by no means comprehensive. Clearly not all clients will respond the same way, and it is therefore important for the worker to individualise the approaches used for each client. (For a more comprehensive, detailed treatment approach, see Berg and Zweben, 1991.)

MANAGEMENT OF DENIAL

Denial of substance use is very common in encounters with clients who show many telltale signs of substance abuse, such as, not paying the rent, no food in the house, accumulated utility bills, and so on. Instead of trying to be subtle about your suspicion of drug or alcohol abuse, a straightforward question asked in the most matter-of-fact manner about their daily use of drugs and alcohol can be useful at times. This must occur after a fair amount of "joining" with the client is done and a good working relationship is established.

Worker: I can see that your life is very stressful. You have many serious problems you have to put up with. And I know that many people in your situation use drugs or drinking to cope with life's difficulties. What do you do that helps you not to use too much drugs or alcohol?"

Discussion:
This normalises the drug and alcohol use, but lets the client know that she has serious problems with which it is difficult to cope. Not only does the worker assume that the client uses drugs or alcohol but the question is how much or how little is used, not whether she uses or not. Drug use is handled as if it is the reasonable thing to do under the circumstances, making the client less defensive in talking about it.

Client: Well, I try to use only a little. I don't use it much. I know I shouldn't but my friends give me some.

Obviously, not all clients respond this way. When they are still sceptical of the worker's motives and deny the problem, the worker still the following options:

a) The worker-team split (see Chapter 9). The primary worker takes the client's side, while the secondary worker or someone else, such as the supervisor, takes a confrontive style.

   Worker: As you know, I have been discussing your situation with my supervisor (or team). He is convinced that there is drug abuse involved here and insists that I am being fooled by you. But I know you are not that kind of person because you have been pretty straight with me. So I don't know what to think. What do you think?

b) The "confusion technique". This puts a lot of pressure on the client, but works well in some cases.

   Worker: As I get to know you, I get a fairly good idea about how difficult your life is. I also have fairly long experience in working with people who use drugs and alcohol. I am confused. Everything about your situation says that you must be using drugs but you are saying you are not using drugs. It just doesn't add up. Maybe you can help me out.

If these methods do not work, you can always try a confrontation of the problems or a urine screening. Some clients will respond better to legal or forceful and demanding approaches. The risk is that you may lose your contact with the client or she may adopt a passive-aggressive stance to deal with your forceful approaches.

CLIENT INVOLVEMENT IN SETTING GOALS

Many studies indicate (Miller, 1985) that when clients participate in setting goals, whatever the problem, and particularly with alcohol abuse, the success rate improves. Therefore, it is important to include the client in setting goals which are small, clear, measurable, and realistic.

Since the FBS program goal is to preserve the family unit while insuring the safety of the children, the worker must always be clear about how the client's drug use enters into and interferes with the client's ability to keep the family together and affects the safety of the children.

The client may sometimes decide on a sporadic use of drugs and/or alcohol and may be reluctant to make a commitment to total abstinence in the beginning.

Although not ideal, it is a worthy goal to pursue because if the client can demonstrate that she can manage her use to a small degree to start with, then she can be helped to increase the period of non-use. It is a small start. If the client cannot maintain a 30-day trial period, then she must confront the reality of dependence.

RELAPSE

Ideally, when a client completes some form of treatment program, she will maintain complete abstinence. However, in reality, both worker and client can expect occasional and periodic setbacks. Expecting and making plans to manage the relapse is not the same as encouraging it. It is prudent and realistic to equip clients with ways to prevent, manage, and control relapse, to recover and "get back on the right track" as soon as possible.

For most abusers and drug dependent persons, stopping using is not hard. They do it every week. Staying sober or clean is the harder task to accomplish. The maintenance of sobriety is often more difficult than "jumping on the wagon". My clinical experience suggests that what the worker does to focus on maintaining sobriety is different from activities directed at prevention of relapse. Membership of the AA, NA, CA (Cocaine Anonymous) or any other self-help group is a good way to maintain sobriety, and to learn a new life-style, which is a difficult task in itself requiring strong support and commitment.

WHAT TO DO IF THERE IS A RELAPSE

Since most experts in the field of alcohol treatment contend that one or two relapses a year are to be considered normal, what should the worker do? The greatest hazard of relapse is the client's own sense of failure and shame at her "weakness" and lack of strong will to live up to her "promise" to herself and to others. It can be quite discouraging for clients, and often they feel that "having to start again" is hopeless and futile. Indeed, such a view can be overwhelming. Clients need help in recognising that a relapse does not mean that they must start over, but that it is a small setback from which they know how to return quite quickly to the previous level of success.

Frequently, a detailed analysis, with the emphasis on future steps, rather than past failures, will point out what the client needs to do differently next time and what strategies she must develop to manage her vulnerable point.

HOW COME THINGS ARE NOT WORSE?

Instead of looking at relapse as a failure, workers can reframe the relapse as her internal reminder that she is still a "recovering person" and that she needs to be more vigilant about her recovery process. The following steps constitute a helpful checklist for the worker when the client reports a relapse.

1. Find out hat it is about this relapse that is different from last time. Any small but significant differences should be noted about each relapse so that client can see

that she is making small but significant progress.

2. Ask how the client managed to stop at the point where she stopped. How did she know to stop at 5 drinks and not go any further? What did she do to stop herself there?
3. What did she learn from this episode that she can apply to the next situation?
4. Find out what the client does between relapses that is good for her. and what she needs "to do more of". They may be such things as: keeping busy, exercising, eating healthily, being productive, etc.
5. Get the client to anticipate the danger points, such as birthdays, parties, outings, holidays, that have previously been occasions for abuse. Devise realistic strategies for non-use.
6. Continue to pay attention to life-style changes, changes of friends, social groups and contacts.
7. Pay attention to the client's larger system issues and watch for the "ripple effects".
8. Continue to support the client through compliments and cheerleading.
9. Reframe the relapse as her unconscious way of reminding herself that she is still an abuser and that she still needs to take "one day at a time".

"THOSE GOD AWFUL CASES"

Thankfully, all workers do not have to mumble these words under their breaths too often but most have said them from time to time. All the wishful thinking that they will disappear is just that, wishful thinking. Even "miracle questions" do not seem to help. It seems that nothing you do helps and you have tried everything you can think of.

What to do if you have one of these cases?

1. Relax You are not alone. Everybody has these cases.

2. Review to check if you have a "customer".

The "customer" may not necessarily be the client. Perhaps it is the court, the school, the disgruntled relative, your supervisor, or even you. Review Chapter 2 for further information.

Case example

The court ordered that Marcus, aged 14, had to be in school, get a job, keep curfew, enroll in a drug treatment program, stay out of trouble with the police, and receive family counselling from the FBS.

The worker discovered that Marcus had a series of difficulties with the court and the school; he was a gang member, most of his friends were in the juvenile correction facility and serving time at such a facility was a badge of honour and a guarantee of admission to the gang; he had not been in school for the past 2 years; his mother was chronically mentally ill; his father was in jail and there had been no contact with the family; there were no relatives who could effectively take control of the family or Marcus. It was not difficult for the worker to see that Marcus' 12-year-old brother was already out of control.

The worker also found that Marcus dealt in drugs, and his income supplemented the AFDC (Aid to Families with Dependent Child) his mother received It was clear that the mother depended on Marcus to supplement this income so that she could buy extra things for the family. Therefore, she was in no position to insist that Marcus stay in school or keep the curfew. Marcus told his mother off at times about her poor parenting. Because she knew that she was dependent on Marcus, mother was cautious and would not discuss her concerns about his future. She was afraid of life without Marcus.

Clearly this was more than a family problem. It was a massive social problem that FBS could not solve. The "customer" here was the community, yet the community was not ready to take action.

With such cases, the worker needs to sort out repeatedly who the "customer" is for which problem.

3. Review to check that you have a customer for change.
With some cases, your job may be to maintain a status quo and not necessarily to make any changes. With these cases your goal may be to act as a case manager, with the emphasis on maintenance, not change.

4. Review to check you have the right goal.
Are you working towards the same goal as the client? Do the clients really want to change or are they saying so because they are trained to say the right words? Clients may need help in sorting out what are realistic goals for their circumstances. Be realistic.

5. Check to see if you have already achieved the goal without knowing it.
Review your initial assessment note and see if you and the client have already achieved the initial goal without being aware of it. You may not have given yourself and the client enough credit for a small success.

6. Make sure that consultation and supervision is available to you.
The availability of formal or peer supervision/consultation on an on-going basis is essential to you. Have brainstorming sessions with your colleagues on those "God awful cases" and get someone else's opinion. Sometimes, it is reassuring to know that your colleagues or supervisors find these cases just as "awful" as you do.

A supportive atmosphere for workers is crucial. There needs to be a regularly scheduled discussion of cases so that helpful techniques can be shared. A certain amount of griping about clients or venting frustration about the system can be helpful at times, but such discussions should not be allowed to turn into regular "bitching sessions". Positive, constructive ideas should emerge from such meetings.

7. Learn from successes and mistakes.

Each family offers us a rich learning experience and we need to be grateful to them for making us feel successful as well as keeping us humble. Analyse your successes as well as mistakes. The common tendency is to focus on failures and mistakes. It is important to know the mistakes but it is also crucial that workers look at what they did right. Keep these successes in mind and apply them to other cases.

8. Remember that you are making a difference in the client's life.

Always remember that you are making a positive difference with every exchange of words, meeting, or contact you have with your client. You are making an important difference in someone's life. That is the most important reward from doing what you are doing. Your professional commitment to helping those who are the most vulnerable, helpless, and in need of our help is remarkable. Keep doing all the good things you are doing.

Bibliography & References

de Shazer, S., (1984). *"The Death of Resistance."* Family Process 23: 79-83

de Shazer, S., (1985). *Keys to Solution in Brief Therapy.* New York: Norton

de Shazer, S., (1988). *Clues: Investigating Solutions in Brief Therapy.* New York: Norton

de Shazer, S., (1991). *Putting Difference to Work.* New York: Norton

de Shazer, S., Berg, I.K., Lipchik, E., Nunnally, E., Molnar, A., Gingerion, W.and Weiner-Davis, M. (1986). *"Brief Therapy: Focused Solution Development"*. Family Process 25: 207-222

DOH (1988). *Protecting Children: A guide for Social Workers Undertaking a Comprehensive Assessment.* HMSO: London

George, E., Iveson, C., Ratner, H. (1990). *Problem to Solution: Brief Therapy with Individuals and Families.* London: BT Press

Kral, R. and Kowalski, K. (1985). *"After the Miracle: The Second Stage in Solution Focused Brief Therapy."* Journal of Strategic and Systemic Therapies, 8 73-76

Lipchik, E. & de Shazer, S., (1986) *"The Purposeful Interview"*. Journal of Strategic and Systemic Therapies 5: 88-99

Lipchik, E. (1988). *"Interviewing with a Constructive Ear."* in Questions in Therapy, Special Edition, Dulwich Centre Newsletter

Nunnally, E., de Shazer, S., Lipchik, E. and Berg, I.K. (1986). *"A Study of Change: Therapeutic Theory in Process"* In (D. Efron, Ed.) Journeys: Expansion of the Strategic-Systemic Therapies. New York: Brunner/Mazey

O'Hanlon, W. and Weiner-Davis, M. (1989). *In Search of Solutions: A New Direction in Psychotherapy.* New York: Norton

White, M. (1988). "The Externalising of the Problem." Dulwich Centre Newsletter, Special Edition

Brief Therapy Books

Norton

Clues – Investigating Solutions in Brief Therapy *Steve de Shazer*   £16.50

Once therapist and client are focused on investigating solutions rather than problems, therapy inevitably becomes brief. Engaging cases, often with surprising twists, illustrate this practice-based theory of brief therapy with a wide range of complaints.

Keys to Solution in Brief Therapy *Steve de Shazer*   £16.50

This book presents an innovative and theoretically elegant approach to brief therapy based on systems theory, the work of Milton Erickson, and the author's many years of experience working with families.

Solution Talk – Hosting Therapeutic Conversations

Ben Furman and Tapani Ahola   £17

"This is a highly readable and clinically practical book which teaches by illustration rather than by theorizing. It should be of interest to many family therapists who, regardless of orientation, have been trying to get away from a pathology orientation in their work." – *AFTA Newsletter*

In Search of Solutions *William Hudson O'Hanlon & Michele Weiner-Davis*   £17

Readers who join O'Hanlon and Weiner-Davis in their search for solutions will find themselves on a path leading towards greater competency and empowerment for both their clients and themselves.

NEW – Two books from Moshe Talmon

Single Session Therapy *Moshe Talmon*   £25.95

Although psychotherapy is often percieved as a long-term process, many clients seeking help attend for one session only – no matter what their therapist's orientation or approach. Moshe Talmon offers a realistic, practical approach to using a single therapeutic session to prompt substantial changes in patients' lives. Rather than suggesting that the therapist condense five or twenty sessions into one, this book shows how to make the most of patients' innate ability to heal themselves – presenting insights into bolstering the patients' existing strengths, restoring autonomy and confidence, and offering solutions that the patient can implement immediately.

Single Session Solutions *Moshe Talmon*   £15.00

This book makes it easier to get into therapy and faster to get out of it. It serves as a unique resource to anyone who can't afford or doesn't want the experience of long-term therapy and for anyone who fears therapy will be a long and interminable road. Moshe Talmon demonstrates how to build a small series of shifts into a crescendo of significant and lasting change: by learning how to steer a session toward solutions, by seeing a therapist as a collaborator instead of as a wise or dominating bestower of answers, by acting as an active and responsible consumer of therapy.

Order by sending to **BT Press, 17 Avenue Mansions, Finchley Road, London NW3 7AX.**
Make cheques payable to 'BT Press' (add 90p for postage & packing).

Divorce Busting *Michele Weiner-Davis* £16.95

Michele Weiner-Davis offers straightfoward advice on staying together, outlines the common illusions of divorce as a solution, and debunks the myth that one's past holds the key to solving problems. Using Solution-Oriented Brief Therapy, she then presents proven marriage-enriching, divorce-prevent techniques based on a simple formula: doing more of what works and less of what doesn't. The focus is on finding solutions – now – for marital discord instead of analysing past problems. With detailed case histories that show the techniques at work.

BT Press

A Field Guide to PossibilityLand *Bill O'Hanlon & Sandy Beadle* £10.00

Possibility Therapy offers a new, more action- and future-oriented approach; a way of encouraging both therapist and client to try out new ideas and new ways to experiment with what works for the client.

Family Preservation – A Brief Therapy Workbook

Insoo Kim Berg, editor Evan George £12.50

The author's work will change practice and will open new solutions for child protection workers who have become dissatisfied with a monitoring role and who are searching for ways to develop co-operation with their clients as a basis for building safety for children. Some chapter headings: What is family based service? / Defining the problem/ Developing cooperation / Setting goals & contracts / Useful questions and other interviewing ideas / Conducting a family session / Do something different / Violence in the family / Alcohol and drug abuse / Those "god-awful cases" / etc.

Problem to Solution – Brief Therapy with Individuals and Families

Evan George, Chris Iveson and Harvey Ratner, foreword by Steve de Shazer £7.50

Introduction to and illustration of a compelling new approach to problem-solving, based on de Shazer's work. It shows how many apparently chronic problems can be quickly and effectively solved by using the client's own aptitudes and strengths. A clear description of the approach and its central interest in exceptions, and how they form the basis of each client's own solution.

Whose Life? – Community Care of Older People and their Families

Chris Iveson £7.95

New, sometimes disturbing, ideas to be used with a minority of clients who take up the majority of time. Illustrates the human & professional dilemmas facing those working with older people, with the stories of clients and their carers is a story of theory-building, particularly around the application of family therapy.

Solution Focused Thinking In Schools *John Rhodes and Yasmin Ajmal* £10.00

How can we find 'Brief' solutions to problems like classroom disruption in schools? How are frustrated teachers to be helped toward a better future with difficult pupils? This book suggests some simple ideas and strategies for finding solutions that work in the context of school. The emphasis is on looking for solution patterns as a basis for rekindling hope and facilitating change. It derives from a perspective which prefers to focus on the present situation and a person's definable goals rather than picking over the past

Moved to Tears, Moved to Action *Jane Lethem* £10.00

The author draws on her experience of Solution Focused Brief Therapy with women and their children to look at case studies through the lens of gender. She illustrates the ways in which its conversational style, emphasis on revealing hidden strengths and potential for tackling social injustice makes Solution Focused Brief Therapy particularly valuable for women.

Dulwich Centre

Re-authoring Lives: Interviews & Essays *Michael White* £14.50

This book makes compelling reading for counsellors, therapists and anyone who is interested in important questions about how people live their lives. You will especially appreciate this book if you are looking for hope and new visions in your work with people who are considered to have chronic problems; are developing ideas for consulting with people who have survived abuse; and if you want to work collaboratively with others in the generation of new possibilities in their lives.

Invitations to Responsibility –
The therapeutic engagement of men who are violent and abusive
Alan Jenkins £14.50

Developing models of intervention that assist abusive males, by helping them to accept responsibility for their actions, to cease abusive behaviours, and relate respectfully to others.

Collected Papers *David Epston* £10.00

Five years of therapeutic cases, written from a personal rather than an objective and scientific viewpoint, and self-consciously concerned with the problems of representation in writing.

Experience, Contradiction, Narrative & Imagination
Epston & White £14.50

A wide-ranging collaboration, covering such subjects as ways of addressing guilt, childhood stealing, dying with AIDS, and self-specialisation.

Pickpockets on a Nudist Camp *Ben Furman & Tapani Ahola* £14.50

Towards a simplification of philosophical discourse surrounding family therapy, taking account of the effect of the observer, and the tyranny of language: "The point is in challenging our way of making sense of what's happening out there."

Selected Papers *Michael White* £10.00

A carefully chosen and representative collection of White's work, the themes of which reflect his interests in constructivism and post-modern thought.

Ideas for Therapy with Sexual Abuse *M. Durrant & C.White, Editors* £14.50

Reflecting the growing awareness of the prevalence of sexual abuse, and suggesting strategies and solutions for therapists that take account of the interaction-within-context approach.

Bedtime Stories for Tired Therapists *ed. Leela Anderson* £14.50

A collection of inspiring an moving accounts of therapists' personal journeys, reflecting on the questions, 'Why do we work in this profession and, given the emotional demands, why do we stay? How does the work challenge and change us, our thinking, our beliefs and our ways•of seeing the world?

BT Press
Newsletters 90-96

Comment

Comment is a new publication initiated to provide a forum for responses to topical social justice issues. It aims to be flexible, open to readers' suggestions and of practical value to health and welfare professionals

1995 No. 2: Homophobia and heterosexual dominance

Challenging heterosexual dominance – the first steps / Speaking out – from the dominant position / The power of language / Are we living in a "gay" new world? / Visibility and invisibility of lesbians within the women's health movement / Working in a straight jacket – the damage done by heterosexual dominance / Lesbians and gays in the classroom / Surviving gay adolescence / Bfriend / Lesbian and gay rights are human rights / Anti-lesbian and gay violence / Discrimination and the law £6.50

Dulwich Centre Newsletters

1995 No. 4:
Speaking out and being heard

The edition of the newsletter is a report that documents the voices of mental health consumers and carers who took part in a joint project that was organised by a group of mental health consumers, carers, the South Australian Council of Social Services (SACOSS) and the Dulwich Centre.

Narrative therapy and its role in the project / Listening to the voices of consumers and carers / Learnings of the listening group members £6.50

1995 No. 2 & 3:
Schooling and Education

The articles in this newsletter raise a variety of challenging questions and provide some stimulating possibilities for action: What implications does an understanding of the dynamics of educational practice have for therapists, counsellors and social workers in their work with families? What are the effects of current practice on individual children, on parents, families and on whole communities? How does schooling fit into larger issues of class, race, gender and sexuality? What

difference would it make if we applied an ethic of care to our thinking about education? How do concepts of accountability relate to adults' relationship with young people, both inside and outside of education?

Schools as communities of acknowledgement *Michael White* / Addressing racism in education *Lester Rigney* / Developing ways of working with young men to reduce violence *David Denborough* / Difference as a source of enrichment *Nguyen Phan Thi Ngoc Dung* / Taking responsibility: working with teasing and bullying in schools *Alice Morgan* / Young people in a context of equity *Leanne Black* / Boys in education in Australia *Christopher McLean* / Conversations with *Noam Chomsky, Lisa Berndt, Phillip Wexler & Shirley Dally* Double issue £11

1995 No. 1: Reclaiming our stories, reclaiming our lives: Counselling in a social justice framework

Many Aboriginal families throughout Autralia have experienced profound grief and pain due to the death in custody of a relative. This newsletter is about the recognition and ongoing need for culturally sensitive and appropriate counselling responses to the needs of these families and communities suffering from the effects of

Order by sending to *BT Press, 17 Avenue Mansions, Finchley Road, London NW3 7AX*.

Make cheques payable to 'BT Press' (add 90p for postage & packing).

such losses, and from the effects of the many injustices that provide a context for these losses.
Deaths in custody / Naming injustice / Narrative Therapy / Why aren't Aboriginal people accessing mainstream services? / Towards culturally appropriate services... / ...what would these services look like... / ...what would make them possible £6.50

1994 No. 4

Challenging developmental truths *Victoria Dickerson, Jeffrey Zimmerman & Lisa Berndt:* Usually ideas of adolescence centre around the task of individuation. This focusses on separation as a metaphor for development. This article proposes a focus on a counter-narrative of connection. It explores the meanings of gender vis-a-vis an understanding of adolescence from a connection metaphor. / **Feminism & postmodernism: Dilemmas and points of resistance** *Rachel Hare-Mustin & Jeanne Marecek:* Feminists were the first to recognise the embeddedness of psychology. Not only is the discipline constituted by its social practices and its location within academia, it reflects and furthers the culture of its time and place. This article looks at the research that is emblematic of American psychology of the last 50 years, and shows how psychology reflects and reaffirms the values of the historical epoch. / **The problem of originality** *David Epston* / **Reflecting Teams: Exploring the possibilities** *Rob Doan & Cassie Bullard:* In its most basic form, the use of a reflective team involves having a team observe a therapy session, and then providing an opportunity for the team to "Gossip in the presence" of the family and therapist. £5.50

1994 No. 2 & 3: New directions for working in partnership

It is extremely difficult for modern Western culture to come to grips with the importance of structured power differences in forming the contexts of people's lives. Western society understands injustice, violence, poverty, racism and sexism as individual aberrations that should be rectifiable with better education and communication skills. "Culture" is seen as vaguely equivalent to "Lifestyle", and concepts such as the "culture of poverty" imply that people basically choose their life situations and are responsible for the consequences. Once we realise how deeply ingrained and culturally influenced our individual ideas and understandings are, it is very difficult to see a way forward. Accountability Structures offer a practical way forward. They start from the recognition of the centrality of structured power differences in our society and develop means of addressing them, so that groups that have been marginalised and oppressed can have their voices heard.
Partnership accountability *Rob Hall* / Pain, hope and heterosexual dominance *Alison Callie* / Adopting the principle of pro-feminism *Ian Law* / A model of hope: Men against sexual assault – Accountability structures *David Denborough* / Cultural & gender accountability in the 'Just Therapy' approach *Kiwi Tamasese & Charles Waldegrave* / A conversation about accountability with Michael White *Christopher McLean* Double issue £10

1993 No. 3 & 4: Professional Sexual Abuse

A survivor of professional sexual abuse was quoted as saying: "Ironically, the aloofness and distance of subsequent psychiatrists has not been helpful to me... Isn't it possible for patient and doctor to treat each other as equals and still distinguish the therapeutic relationship from the social one?".
Empowering clients who have been abused by therapists *Sarah Calvert* / A survivor's long struggle for justice *Jeany Marshall & David Epston* / Moving from victim/survivor to "activityist" *Melissa Roberts-Henry* / When intimacy goes awry *Estelle Disch* / A case of therapist abuse of a patient *Rachel T. Hare-Mustin* / Toward collaboration & accountability *Dean Lobovits & Jennifer C. Freeman* / Response to 'Toward collaboration & accountability' *Anne Jauregui* / The ethics of dual relationships *Karl Tomm* / Common errors in treatment of victims/survivors *Gary Richard Schoener* / Betrayal – clergy sexual abuse & male survivors *Walter H. Bera* / A systems perspective on sexual exploitation of clients by professional helpers *William White* Double issue £10

1993 No. 2

Exploring stories of Lesbian experiences in therapy *Kathleen Stacy:* Homophobia, wittingly or unwittingly may have contributed to the comparative paucity of the publication of lesbian experience within family therapy contexts. This article helps therapists orient themselves to being more confortable in talking with clients who wish to bring their lebian experiences to therapy. / **Heterosexual dominance in the world of therapy?** *Daphne Hewson:* A reflective ramble through the personal experiences and

Order by sending to BT Press, 17 Avenue Mansions, Finchley Road, London NW3 7AX.
Make cheques payable to 'BT Press' (add 90p for postage & packing).

current perspective of a therapist considering the heterosexual dominance of therapy. / **Don't leave mother in the waiting room** Margret Roberts / **Internalised other questioning of men who are violent** David Nylund & Victor Corsiglia: This article discusses therapy with mothers and children, following the disclosure of child sexual assault perpetrated by a person related to the child. / **Comments on 'Internalised other questioning'** Alan Jenkins: How to facilitate the process of abusive males learning to move beyond *thinking* about to *feeling* about, the potential impact of their abusive behaviour. / **Imaginary friends** Emily Betterton as told to David Epston / **The narrative job interview** Cassie Bullard & Don Clifton: "Everybody rises to their own level of incompetence". Therapists who attain enough responsibility to interview potential employees can be invited to feel that they have reached this dreaded level. This article suggests some elements of a "Therapy Test" / Acknowledging Karl Tomm David Epston   £5.50

1993 No. 1:
Colonisation & Family Therapy

This is a story of an encounter between two ends of the world who came together to share stories of subjugation, dispossession and alienation under their colonial past, and to explore therapeutic solutions to the present difficulties of their people. It was a workshop presented by workers of the Family Centre of New Zealand for the Mid-Island Tribal Council - a council representing four of the tribes of Native North American people. This issue goes beyond the proceedings of the workshop to provide readers with a broader perpective on the historical and political perspective which made such a workshop necessary. Colonialism – Then and now / Residential schools – the pain and shame / In search of a 'Just Therapy' – the mid-island tribal council context / Pura pura tuku iho – the seed that has been passed down / Gender – the impact of western definitions of womanhood on other cultures / Behind the one-way mirror / The secular and the Spiritual – a collision of worlds Carmel Tapping / Resonances April Boyd   £5.50

1992 No. 3 & 4: Men's ways of being

The "discovery" and articulation of men's pain has been one of the central motivating forces of the men's movement since the 1970s. Is it legitimate for men to even think about their own pain while women continue to experience such horrific levels of violence? Are they continuing the age-old pattern of male self-centeredness? Or is a denial of pain one of the building blocks of the oppression of women?

Dichotomies in the making of men Gregory Smith / Men's culture, the men's movement and the constitution of men's lives Michael White / Father and father on Graham Harbord / Healing the mother wound Maggie Carey / Perspectives on the men's movement Maggie Carey / The politics of gender Ian Law   £8.50

1992 No. 2: Women

The secret hero sings... Where are all the secret witnesses? Anonymous / Grandmothers or witches: Images of older women Judith Cross / The traps that come with the trappings: A conversation with Lillian Holt Carmel Tapping / A vision for women's studies at university Anna Yeatman / Unique outcomes or intimate immensity Carol Kayrooz / From debate to dialogue: A facilitating role for family therapists in the public forum Sallyann Roth, Laura Chasin, Richard Chasin, Carol Becker & Margaret Herzig / A decade of woman in family therapy meetings Susi Chamberlain£5.50

1992 No. 1

Owning one's epistemological stance in therapy James Griffith & Melissa Griffith / Exposing secret biographies Sasha Pilkington & Nicky Fraser / Schizophrenia from the inside out Michael Lee / Theory countertransference Mark Hubble & Bill O'Hanlon / Discourse not language: The shift from a modernist view of language to the postmodern analysis of discourse in family therapy Ian Law & Stephen Madigan / Authors and re-authoring Sue Park & Jenny Baker / Marry me, marry my profession Claire Miran Khan £5.50

1991 No. 4: Schizophrenia – Some Views & Experiences

It is difficult to know whether to speak of patients, clients, customers, sufferers or persons with schizophrenia. This conundrum reflects the many different views about schizophrenia, each view partial, biased and political.

Psychiatric practice and the definition of schizophrenia Robert Barrett / Like mother like daughter Marina Gloster / Changes in mental health policy and their effects on the treatment of severe mental disorders: Findings from the Italian experience Germana Agnetti & Angelo Barbato / A

Order by sending to BT Press, 17 Avenue Mansions, Finchley Road, London NW3 7AX.

Make cheques payable to 'BT Press' (add 90p for postage & packing).

practical model for treating schizophrenia in the real world *Margaret Newmark* / Challenging the dominant story: Behind the "worthy of discussion" groups *Carmel Tapping* / Consumer participation in psychiatric services: The myth can be a reality *Terry Melbourne* / Them and us: Can we co-operate? *Michael Dugan and others*   £5.50

Living with HIV and AIDS *Jeffrey Lipp* / Dying and AIDS *Michael White & David Epston* / Women and AIDS *Carmel Tapping* / The growing edge of client care *Gabe Phillips* / Overcoming prejudice through education and support *Kay Slaytor & Kate Henderson* / Review of the film "A Death in the Family" *Banu Maloney*   £5.50

1991 No. 3: Postmodernism, Deconstruction & Therapy

It seems that however powerful a client may be in their own contexts, they assume that the therapist is an expert at resolving certain kinds of problems. The process of giving and receiving the authority to do therapeutic work can be seen as being closely akin to the invocation of the Oracle. The task of the oracle is to pronounce with the authority of the gods upon the lives of humans, and by pronouncing, change those lives. From laboratory to therapy room: Prediction questions for constructing the 'new-old' story *Daphne Hewson:* This article shows how therapists can practically apply in therapy ideas that arise from the theoretical awareness made available by postmodernism. / **Situating therapist questions in the presence of the family** *Stephen Madigan:* It is no longer sufficient to passively accept the mantle of the Oracle. The therapist must be prepared to be self-reflexive in public as well as in private. / **Deconstruction and therapy** *Michael White:* By working with clients and reflecting teams in the co-authoring of new narratives for both clients and therapists, the mask of the Oracle is permanently set aside. / **Postmodern themes and therapeutic parctices** *Roger Lowe:* Is postmodernism useful in family therapy? Is there a danger of postmodernism becoming a "new totalising metanarrative" - i.e. replacing one set of absolute truths with a novel form of an essentially familliar foundationalism? Is postmodernism not only politically ambivalent, but potentially politically disempowering?   £5.50

1991 Vol 2: Living with HIV and AIDS

This edition speaks with personal, professional and political voices. It developed out of a growing awareness of the impact AIDS is having on us, both as therapists and as people. We are working with those who have an infection for which there is yet no cure, who live with an all-pervading uncertainty, and those who are dying before their time. It is not possible to work with those affected by HIV and AIDS without being affected personally.

1991 No. 1: Men's Experience of Men's Culture

The objectives for this edition are to offer articles that show men striving to discover caring sensitive and respectful roles for themselves; to describe many options for men, rather than being prescriptive and suggesting that there is a particular "right" way for men to be; and to offer a broad base of men's experience of patriarchy.

Reflections of a man who practices sexual therapy *Gary Sanders* / Birthing *Malcolm Walker* / Benny the peanut man *David Epston* / AIDS - a gay lesson in caring *Gary Dowsett* / What's a nice woman like me doing in a place like this? *Dallas Colley* / Personal and political responses to a patriarchal culture *Dob Gobbet* / Growing up as a man *Peter Lee* / On being a single father *Peter Bleby* / Review of the film "Pretty Woman" *Alan Jenkins* / How does this bit work, Dad? *Iain Lupton*   £5.50

1990 No. 1: Social Justice and Family Therapy

The work of The Family Center, New Zealand has broken new ground in the Western world by developing a therapy that addresses issues of colonisation, gender, culture, class, poverty and spirituality. The team do more than practice a model of social justice, they live it. In providing this model of social justice, they hold up a mirror for us to see the areas in our own culture where there are inequities.

What is Just Therapy? / Weaving threads of meaning/ Socio-economic context / When working with men who abuse / The therapeutic exchange *Charles Waldegrave* Culturally appropriate therapy / Colonisation and its effects / Research and political involvement / Men for Non-violence / The story of the Samoan people / Spirituality *Carmel Tapping*   £5.50

Order by sending to *BT Press, 17 Avenue Mansions, Finchley Road, London NW3 7AX.*
Make cheques payable to 'BT Press' (add 90p for postage & packing).